Published by Aperitifs Publishing Company
Santa Rosa, California

Copyright: March 2023
Written by: Tim Higgins

Compiled & Published by John C. Burton
johncburton@msn.com
707-523-1611

ISBN: 978-1-7324530-7-4
Library of Congress Number: 2023903378

Printed in the United States of America

All rights reserved. No part of this book may be reproduced or transformed in any form or by any means, electronic or mechanical, including photocopying, recording or by any information storage and/or retrieval system without permission in writing from the publisher.

I, John C. Burton, on September 23, 2022, purchased the contents and rights to this publication from Tim Higgins of Jackson, California.

Tim Higgins, made every attempt to provide accurate information on the following subjects.

FRONT COVER ACKNOWLEDGEMENTS

S. F. BADER & Co. XLCRSODA WORKS	Eric McGuire FOHBC Regional Director
DITZ & ELLERKAMP SAN FRANCISCO	Eric McGuire FOHBC Regional Director

REAR COVER ACKNOWLEDGEMENTS

BOLEY & Co. SAC. CITY CAL.	Jeff Wichmann American Bottle Auctions
HUMBOLDT SODA NATURAL MINERAL WATER	California State Archives Old Trademarks
CALIFORNIA SODA WORKS (Branches) H. FICKEN S.F.	Jeff Wichmann American Bottle Auctions
EXCELSIOR SODA & MINERAL WATER FACTORY	Eddie Kuskie Collector Extraordinaire
NEW ALMADEN VICHY WATER CALIFORNIA	Eric McGuire FOHBC Regional Director
BABB & Co. SAN FRANCISCO, CAL.	Jeff Wichmann American Bottle Auctions

SPECIAL APPRECIATION TO

Special appreciation to Peck & Audie Markota's daughter Jeanne Deschamps and granddaughter Julie Youngblood for allowing us to reference and reprint with updates and additions, WESTERN BLOB TOP SODA AND MINERAL WATER BOTTLES book. That book is our inspiration. JB

Mike Southworth who I met in September 2022 at the Santa Rosa Bottle Show and started me on this journey of reprinting Peck & Audie Markota's book.

CONTENTS

A TRIBUTE TO PECK MARKOTA	
ACKNOWLEDGMENTS 3rd EDITION	I
ADDITIONAL ACKNOWLEDGMENTS	II
FORWARD	III
ORIGINAL BOTTLE LISTINGS	1-105

ADDITIONS BY MIKE SOUTHWORTH:

John S. Baker Mineral Water	Pages 4A & 4B
Deamer & Bordwell	23A & 23 B
Golden West Soda	37 A
Asher S. Taylor	85 A
BOTTLES BY GROUPS	106
ORIGINAL INDEX	107-108

Markota's book(s) are valuable references but was completed before the use of computers as we know them today. Jeff Wichmann's American Bottle Auction catalogs are too valuable to waste the excellent photos of rare bottles.

With the additional listings of unlisted bottles from the collections of Mike Southworth, John O'Neill, John Louder, Richard Siri and Rick Siri it places more information into this endeavor.

That being said; I consolidated the information presented in each book and have created a reference guide in color to assist local collectors.

With special appreciation to Peck & Audie Markota's daughter Jeanne Deschamps and granddaughter Julie Youngblood for allowing us to reference and reprint with additions, WESTERN *BLOB TOP SODA AND MINERAL WATER BOTTLES* book. That book was our inspiration. JB

A TRIBUTE TO PECK MARKOTA

One of bottle collecting's most prominent and well-liked members died October 3 from heart and kidney complications, Stephen "Peck" Markota was a mainstay of the hobby and good friend to everyone. He was 76.

Peck, as we all called him, was a man who not only loved collecting bottles and other assorted things, he also was a man who spent much of his adult life spreading the word and working to further his fascination and love for antique bottles. He and his wonderful wife, Audie, wrote the definitive book on western soda bottles and then another on California Hutchinson bottles. He started the first bottle show in the Sacramento area in Folsom on June 14, 1969. This set the stage for others who would follow and begin setting up their own shows throughout the state. Among his many achievements, he was elected the Federation of Historic Bottle Collectors second vice chairman of the first FOHBC board of directors at the 1969 meeting in Berkeley. He was also elected 1st vice chairman of FOHBC at the convention in Denver in 1969. A member of 11 different bottle clubs, a tireless bottle exhibitor and author, his enthusiasm for the hobby never waned. As well-known bottle guru Bill Baab wrote in 2006, "In nearly every club, there is a nucleus of a few members who do all the work needed to keep it going, while the rest of the membership are content to do nothing. Meet Peck Markota, one of the workhorses of the Federation." Peck was eventually elected to the FOHBC Hall of Fame in 1993 and was the Federation's first Honorary Director. As many have said, it was Peck who was the true spark behind the Federation being founded.

Most of all, it was Peck the nice guy. Peck, who would talk about his kids, grandchildren and great grandchildren as if they were angels, sent to earth. He never had a bad word to say about anyone and that's the truth. When someone passes on, we hear the most wonderful things about them regardless of whom they were. I can assure you that everything people will say about Peck from here on is the truth. When I started my antique bottle auctions, I wasn't exactly welcomed with open arms. The first National show I went to I felt quite awkward and a little out of place. Who came up to me and introduced me to the mainstays of the hobby? You guessed it. Peck judged people by who they were not what he'd heard. If somebody had something bad to say about someone else, Peck would just as soon walk away and start a discussion with another friend. He was opinionated but his wonderful smile and generous demeanor were only stoking a friendly fire. He wanted so badly to share his passion and love of the hobby, he literally spent much of his life doing just that.

Goodbye, old friend, I still say your name almost every day as I write my bottle descriptions and talk about sodas. A day before he died, I was doing the soda section of our upcoming auction and like every auction, without Peck and Audie's book, I'd be lost. Markota this, Markota that, his quest for knowledge never stopped, thank goodness. His legacy will live on; it's in so many of us who were lucky enough to know him. He never stopped giving and now we'll never stop remembering him. Peck Markota, a great man and bottle pioneer. The hobby wouldn't be the same without you and that my friend will be true forever. Goodbye.

Sincerely, Jeff Wichmann

ACKNOWLEDGMENTS

This page of acknowledgements is for the original 2005 Third Edition. They are listed alphabetically, as it was impossible to measure each individuals contribution. This book would not have been possible without all the help from the following people.

WARREN BORTON, MIDVALE, UT.
CHRISTIAN BUYS, GRAND JUNCTION, COLO.
FRANK & JUDY BROCKMAN, STOCKTON, CA.
RON CECIL, STOCKTON, CA.
MIKE DOLCINI, SACRAMENTO, CA.
DAVE EMMITT, SALT LAKE CITY, UT.
RON FOWLER, SEATTLE, WASH.
MIKE GASTALDI, CAMINO, CA.
BRYAN GRAPENTINE, PHOENIX, AZ.
JACK GIBSON, CARSON CITY, NV.
CRAIG GILDART, CITRUS HEIGHTS, CA.
BEVERLY GILLASPY, RED BLUFF, CA.
DOUG HANSEN, REDDING, CA.
FRED HOLABIRD, RENO, NV.
RALPH HOLLIBAUGH, REDDING, CA.
MARK HUDDLESTON, SAN JOSE, CA.
GORDON HUGI JR., ROUGH & READY, CA.
TOM JACOBS, SAN RAFAEL, CA.
JEFF JOHNSON, LITTLETON, COLO.
JESS JONES, BELMONT, CA.
JEFF KAYE, BLUE LAKE, CA.
DAN KEENER, OGDEN, UT.
ERIC McGUIRE, MILL VALLEY, CA.
JOHNNY PLAYER, SALT LAKE CITY, UT.
BRUCE RINGSMITH, NAPA, CA.
KEN SALAZAR, SAN FRANCISCO, CA.
DANETTE SCROGGINS, SACRAMENTO, CA.
JACOB SCROGGINS, SACRAMENTO, CA.
STEPANIE SCROGGINS, SACRAMENTO, CA.
RANDY TAYLOR, CHICO, CA.
JOHN THOMAS, WEAVERVILLE, CA.
ALLEN WILSON, MONTELLO, NV.
BETTY ZUMWALT, SAND POINT, ID.

THANK YOU ALL VERY MUCH,
Peck and Audie Markota

ACKNOWLEDGMENTS

This page of acknowledgements is for the revised 2020 edition. I would like to thank American Bottle Auctions and Glass Works Auctions for many of the photos, and auction pricing. And a special thanks to Max Bell for the use of his research into the Golden Gate soda. Also to Mike Southworth for upgrading some of my bad pictures with some photos from his superb collection of western sodas. Warren Friedrich supplied the updated information on the earliest pontled sodas.

DAN BELL, AUBURN, CA.
MAX BELL, AUBURN, CA.
JOHN BURTON, SANTA ROSA, CA.
RON CECIL, STOCKTON, CA.
TOM CHAPMAN, BIG PINE, CA.
WARREN FRIEDRICH, GRASS VALLEY, CA.
RICK HALL, SAN DIEGO, CA.
DOUG HANSON, PALO CEDRO, CA.
MIKE HENNESS, IONE, CA.
FRED HOLABIRD, RENO, NV.
DONALD KING, BENICIA, CA.
ANDREW KOUTSOUKOS, SAN RAFAEL, CA.
RICK LINDGREN, MARTINEZ, CA.
TOM QUINN, BENICIA, CA.
JAMES QUINN, BENICIA, CA.
CY ROLLINS, GOODYEARS BAR, CA.
RICK SIMI, DOWNIEVILLE, CAL.
MIKE SOUTHWORTH, UPLAND, CA.
JEFF WICHMAN, SACRAMENTO, CA.

And another special thanks to all the bottle diggers and collectors who inspired Peck and Audie Markota to research and write this great book. It has been the go-to source for information on Western Sodas since the day it was completed. It has been an honor for me to update it.

Tim Higgins
Jan. 2020

FORWARD

Explanation of terminology and abbreviations, etc. used in this book.

A / following a word denotes a new line of embossing

A " around" a word denotes an embossed picture, such as an "EAGLE"

A.T. denotes Applied Top

T.T. denotes Tooled Top

I.P. denotes Iron Pontil Base

S.B. denotes Smooth Base

O.P. denotes Open Pontil Base

Shape of the bottle is denoted by Round, 8 Sided, 10 Sided, etc.

Locality: area where the bottle was originally distributed, not necessarily found.

Circa: Dates were from when the bottle was used by the manufacturer. This could vary greatly by the bottle being purchased from a used bottle dealer and then reused by another bottler. So we tried to go by the dates the original bottler was in business.

Rarity: Here is the Rarity scale used,

Ex. Rare	10 or Less
Rare	10 to 30
Scarce	30 to 50
Common	50 plus

In my opinion Soda type bottles should have a much different rarity scale than lets say a Bitters or a Whiskey bottle. They were generally ordered in much larger quanities and many were reused many times before being discarded. They did tend to survive longer than other types of bottles. This scale was put together by many prominent collectors and diggers.

Value: The pricing listed is actual auction selling prices and the year sold. These are from American Bottle Auctions and Glass Works Auctions. They are for a near mint bottle unless otherwise stated. Many things effect value, especially on a soda bottle. Wear from usage being a major factor, as some were reused many times. Color and crudity also effect value. You could have a common bottle in aqua and if it came in cobalt blue, it would be much more valuable. Condition issues such as chips and cracks will bring any bottles value down. Bottles from certain areas may be worth more locally than to a collector in another area of the state. Same goes for bottles from lets say Utah, being more valuable to Utah collectors that someone in California. But the only real true value is what someone is willing to pay for it.

History: Much of this info is from old business directories, newspaper and other similar means. A lot of time was spent to try to make it as accurate as possible. There are bound to be some inaccuracy in the dates and history due to directories we could not access, and some that did not even get published.

Front: AETNA / MINERAL WATER
Re: NATURAL / MINERAL WATER

Front: AETNA / MINERAL WATER
Re: AETNA / MINERAL WATER

Front: AETNA / SODA WATER
Re: NATURAL / MINERAL WATER

Front: AETNA / MINERAL WATER / TRADE MARK / REGISTERED
Re: AETNA / MINERAL WATER / TRADE MARK / REGISTERED
Base: AETNA

Round, Smooth base
Tooled and Applied Top
Aqua, Lime Green, Amethyst
Common in Aqua, Amethyst
Rare in Lime Green
Circa: 1886-1905
Locale: San Francisco
Note: Bottle #2 comes with an Applied Top. The "Aetna Mineral Water" and "Aetna Soda Water" name were trade marked in 1887. The "Aetna Ginger Ale" name was trade marked in 1888 by Len Owens, S.F. See at Right.

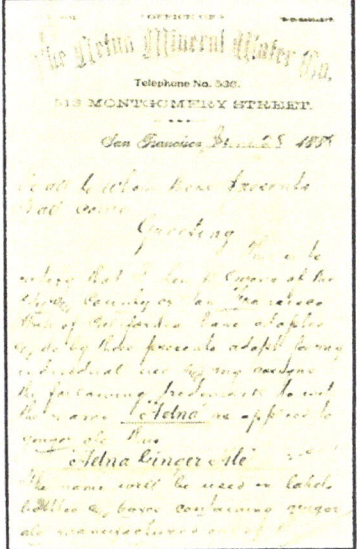
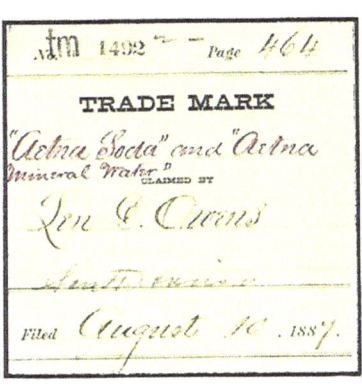

HISTORY: Aetna Mineral Springs is located in Pope Valley, about 15 miles east of St. Helena. Most of the original buildings of the resort are still standing as of 2018. In 1886 the springs was owner by Hon. Chancellor Hartson of Napa.

1886-1887 Aetna Mineral Springs, A.F. Learned Agent, Office and Depot, 757 ½ Howard
1887-1888 Aetna Mineral Springs, A.F. Cooper Agent, 757 ½ Howard
1888-1889 Aetna Mineral Water from the Aetna Springs, Napa Co. Cal., Owens and Bartlett Agents, Office 513 Montgomery, Warehouse 57 Clay, Tel. 536
1889-1899 Aetna Mineral Water Co., L.D. Owen President, John J. O'Brien Secretary, Office and Warehouse 106-108 Drumm, Tel. 536
1899-1900 Aetna Mineral Water Co., John. J. O'Brien President, Mineral Water from the Aetna Springs, Linn & Klee Sole Agents, 619 Montgomery, Tel. Main 1729
1900-1901 Aetna Mineral Water, Louis Klee & Co. Sole Agents U.S., 604-608 Bryant
1901-1902 Aetna Mineral Water, Baumgarten & Co. Sole Agents U.S., 604-608 Bryant
1902-1903 No Listing
1903-1904 Aetna Mineral Water Agency, No. 7 10th
1904-1905 Aetna Mineral Water Agency, Hilbert Mercantile Co. Agents, 213 Market
1905 Aetna Mineral Water Agency, 140 2nd
No Further Listings

Front: SODA WATER / ULR ALTING

Round Torpedo, Smooth Base
Applied Top
Deep Olive Green, $4600.00 - 1997
Ex. Rare
Circa: 1849-1851
Locale: Honolulu, Hawaii
Note: The Alting bottles have only been found in the Islands so far.

HISTORY: Ulrich Alting was in the general merchandise business in Honolulu in the late 1840's. Early records have no mention of him being in the soda water business at this time. He took on a partner some time in 1850. Edward Heeren was a ship captain and they entered a partnership in Dec. 1850. The partnership ended in 1851 and Alting continued on with his general merchandise business. In his ads he stated that he had for sale a "large soda water machine, complete with bottles, corks, etc". This is surely proof that Alting and Heeren were bottling soda water. Further proof is that about one later Edward Heeren ran an ad stating that he was manufacturing soda water. He must have purchased Alting's machine after the partnership dissolved. Alting left Hawaii in late 1851.

Front: ULR ALTING / SPARKLING / LEMONADE

Round, Smooth Base
Applied Top
Deep Olive Green
Ex. Rare
Circa: 1849-1851
Locale: Honolulu, Hawaii

HISTORY: See above bottle

Front: AMERICAN / "FLAG" / MINERAL WATER CO. / S.F.

Round, Smooth Base
Tooled Top
Aqua, Lime Green
Ex. Rare
Varient: Hutch and Crown Top
Circa: 1899-1906
Locale: San Francisco
Note: Trade Marked in 1899 by Rooney & Zimmerman S.F. See drawing at right.

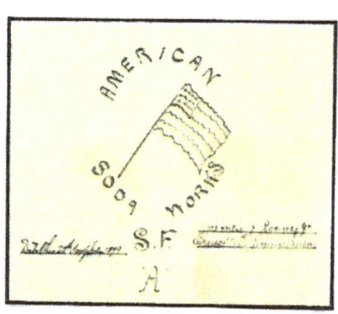

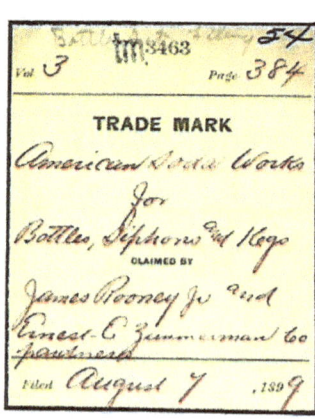

HISTORY: From 1899 thru 1915, James J. Rooney and Ernest Zimmerman were the proprietors of the American Soda Water Works, with their place of business at 924 Bryant St. from 1899 to 1905, and at 2485 Bryant St. from 1905 to 1915.

Front: ASTORG / MINERAL / WATER

   Round, Smooth Base
   Tooled Top
   Aqua, $250.00 - 2017
   Rare
   Varient: Hutch
   Circa: 1896-1906
   Locale: San Francisco

HISTORY: Alphonse Astorg, a butcher and meat market owner for many years, discovered a spring in Cobb Valley, Lake County Cal. and appropriately named it Astorg Mineral Springs. Alphonse bottled this new found water and sold it at his meat market, which was located at 108 Fifth St. in S.F., from 1896 to 1906.

Front: "AZULE" / SELTZER / SPRINGS
Re: TRADE / "BEAR" / MARK

   Round, Smooth Base
   Applied Top
   Aqua, $325.00 - 2021
   Lime Green
   Scarce in Aqua
   Ex. Rare in Green
   Circa: 1885-1890
   Locale: Santa Clara, Cal.
   Note: Label Trade Marked in 1892 by
      Azule Seltzer Water Co. These bottles
      are usually found in the San Jose area,
      Santa Cruz and Watsonville have
      yielded a few.

HISTORY: Luther Mills sold the Mills Seltzer Springs to John Ryland, in 1885, and he renamed it Azule Seltzer Springs.

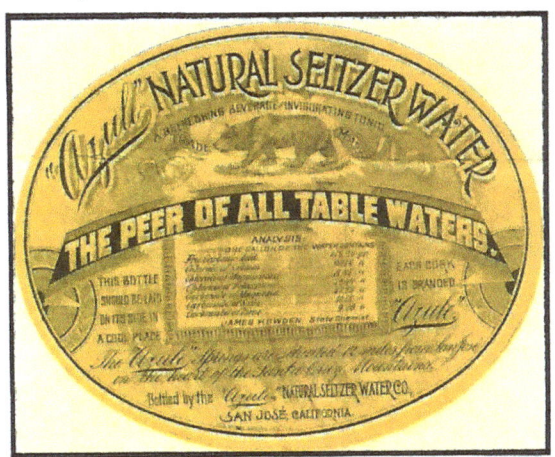

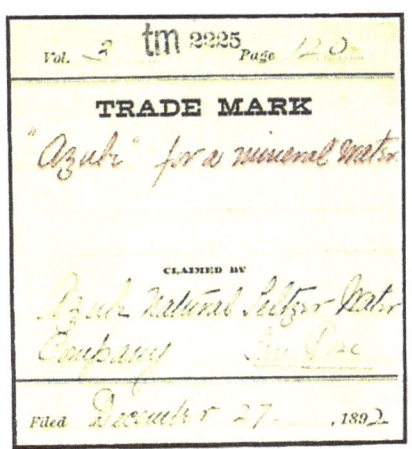

Front: B (block letter)

Round, Smooth Base
Applied Top
Aqua
Common
Varient: Hutch and Crown Top
Circa: 1871-1885
Locale: Stockton and Marysville, Cal.
Note: This bottle is usually found in many of the towns along the Sacramento and San Joaquin rivers in the central valley of California. One was dug in Vacaville in 1977 and also in Vallejo in 1980.

HISTORY: Charles Belding came to Stockton sometime in 1854 and entered employment with the soda water manufacturer Lippincott and Vaughn. In 1856, Belding went back east, he returned in 1857 and bought a part ownership in his old company, then becoming Lippincott & Belding. This lasted until 1870, when Belding bought out Lippincott's share.

Stockton
1870-1895 Charles Belding, Soda Water manufacturer and Ins. Agent, cor. Weber and San Joaquin St. Stockton
1895-1900's Belding & Huskin, Soda Water manufacturers, 303 E. Weber Ave.

Marysville
1870-1875 Charles Belding, Soda Water manufacturer, Cor. Second and Virgin Alley
1875-1885 Lyman Belding, Proprietor Marysville Soda Works, Cor. Second & Virgin Alley. (Lyman was Charles Belding's brother)
1885-1900's Charles Belding Soda Works, Second between B and C Sts.
See also Lippincott & Vaugh, Lippincott & Belding

Front: BABB & CO. / SAN FRANCISCO / CAL.

Round, Iron Pontil
Applied Top
Blue Aqua, $425.00 - 2008
Deep Green, $600.00 - 2017
Green, $550.00 - 2021
Teal, $350.00 - 2021
Scarce
Circa: 1852-1854
Locale: San Francisco
Note: This bottle has been found in the San Francisco redevelopment areas in the 1960's and 70's. A few have come out of Gold Rush era mining camps in Placer and Nevada counties. One was dug in a privy in Benicia in 1976, and a few have come out of the Benicia mud flats over the years.

HISTORY: Jeffries Babb arrived in San Francisco in 1851. In 1852 and 1853, Babb & Co. were listed as soda Water manufacturers at 384 Stockton St. In 1854, Babb & Co. were listed as a Soda Water Factory at 280 Dupont St. Being that there was no S.F. city business directory for 1855, he could have been in business for another year.

John S. Baker
Sacramento
c.1853-1857
Comes in both aqua and green
Embossing two variants

JOHN S. BAKER/ MINERAL WATERS/ THIS BOTTLE IS NEVER/ SOLD

JOHN S. BAKER/ SODA WATER/ THIS BOTTLE/ IS NEVER SOLD
(Smaller font)

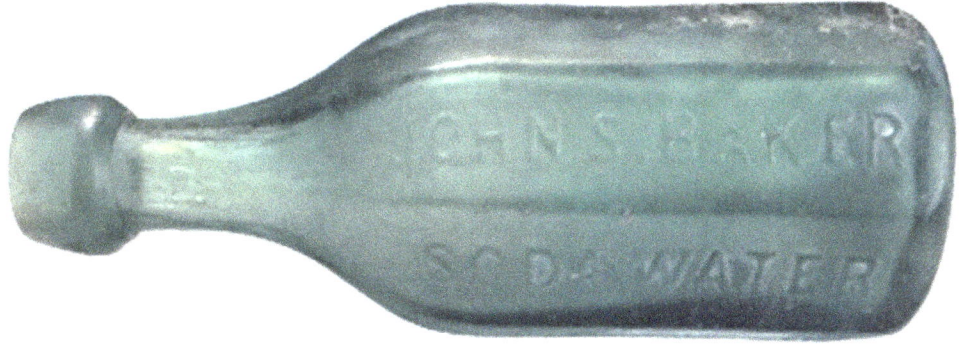

Above images Mike Southworth collection

Addendum 4-A

Sacramento Union
February 17, 1853

ATROCIOUS HIGHWAY ROBBERY

Mr. Alleman, of the firm of Alleman & Baker, soda manufacturers of this city, received intelligence, by a gentleman who came down from Nevada on Wednesday, to the startling effect:

Mr. John S. Baker, his partner, started on horseback for Nevada on Thursday. When on the road, somewhere in the vicinity of the ten- or fifteen-mile house, two horsemen, whom he recognized as Americans, rode up and joined him. The party cultivated a conversational acquaintance, and were proceeding on the journey for an hour or more in company.

At a spot in the road where no teams or persons where in view, one of the horsemen spurred his animal suddenly forward, and demanded of Mr. Baker in an authoritative tone to follow him, while the other reined his stead in, an fell back, drawing a revolver at the same time, and reiterating the command. Mr. Baker was totally unarmed, and had no alternative but to obey. The horsemen made a detour from the road to a short distance of, when Mr. Baker was ordered to deliver over his money and other valuables, on pain of having his brains blown out. He had with him about a hundred dollars, a watch and a breast pin, of which the robbers relieved him, after they forced him to dismount. They tied his hands behind his back, and his legs together near the ankles. This done they stripped his horse of its furniture, turned it loose, and rode off.

Mr. Baker succeeded in drawing one foot out of his boot, by which his legs were rendered free. He ran back to the road, where he met several teams, whose drivers were made acquainted with his story. They released his arms, and requesting one of their number to take charge of the teams, went with Mr. Baker to assist him in catching his horse.

Article forwarded by Mike Southworth
California Digital Newspaper

Please note the wording of the day; "This done they stripped his horse of its furniture," meaning saddle, bridle and blanket.

Addendum 4-B

Front: BAY CITY SODA WATER / CO. / S.F.
Re: "STAR"

Round, Smooth Base
Applied Top
Cobalt, $375.00 - 2017
Teal Blue, $750.00 - 2017
Teal Green, $950.00 - 2017
Cobalt with Olive, $1800.00 - 2021
Common in Shades of Blue
Rare in other Colors
Circa: 1871-1880
Variant: no "STAR" on reverse, Rare
Varient: Hutch
Locale: San Francisco
Note: Bottle trade marked in
    1872 by James McEwin S.F.
    See drawing at right

HISTORY: The Bay City Soda Water Co. was incorporated in 1871 and was in business until 1913. Trustees were John Rohe, Cephas Turner, H.P. Rice, Henry Brader, Benjamin Ellerkamp, James Blevin and James McEwin. In that time they moved their operations six times.

- 1871-1878, James McEwin president, 89 Stevenson
- 1878-1881, James McEwin president, 110 Tyler
- 1881-1895, James McEwin president, 110-112 Golden Gate Ave.
- 1895-1897, Henry A. Cline president, 116-118 Golden Gate Ave.
- 1897-1906, Henry A. Cline president, 117-123 Hyde St.
- 1906-1913, Henry A. Cline, 320 Fell St.

The Company went out of business some time in 1913.

Front BELFAST / TRADE "B in TRIANGLE" MARK / GINGER ALE CO. / S.F.

Round, Smooth Base
Tooled Top
Aqua
Ex. Rare
Varient: without CO., Hutch and Crown Top
Circa: 1881-1920+
Locale: San Francisco

HISTORY: On Nov. 5, 1877 John Chambers of the Pacific Mineral Water Co. applied for and received a trade mark for Belfast Ginger Ale. Label above. Alexander Chambers and Thomas Pyne were co-owners of the Pacific Mineral Water Co., which was listed as the manufacturer of Belfast Ginger Ale at 1637 Howard St. Chambers and Pyne stayed together at the Howard location until 1881 when Pyne decided to try it solo. After 1881 the building of the soda works began to fall apart, first Pyne moved from the Howard location to a building at the rear of 145 Valencia, next he changed the name to the Belfast Ginger Ale Co. Everything for Pyne went downhill after 1886 when he was listed as just being a clerk. Pyne tried an unsuccessful come back in 1888 by manufacturing soda water for the next couple of years at different locations in the city. In 1888 Frederick and Richard Steimke converted their building on the corner of Octavia and Union Sts into the Belfast Ginger Ale Co. The name was used earlier by others and we have no idea why the Steimke Bros. decided to reuse the name, which had a trade mark on it, unless they purchased it from John Chambers, who had acquired it in 1877. This time around for the Belfast Ginger Ale Co. must have been a super successful business, staying at the 2769 Octavia address for over 33 years until 1921. The company also stayed in the control of the Steimke family for the entire time the bottling works was in business.

Front: BELFAST / GINGER ALE CO.
Re: SAN FRANCISCO / CAL.

Round, Smooth Base
Applied Top
Deep Aqua, $700.00 - 2017
* $500.00 - 2009*
Rare
Circa: 1877-1881 (approx)
Locale: San Francisco

HISTORY: See above bottle

Front E.L. BILLINGS / SAC CITY
Re: GEYSER SODA

Round, Smooth Base
Applied Top
Yellow Green, $1700.00 - 2021
Lime Green, $400.00 - 2010
Aqua, $140.00 - 2010
Blue, $325.00 - 2021
Deep Lime Green, $3200.00 - 2009
Blue Aqua, $90.00 - 2021
Lt. Green, $240.00 - 2021
Circa: 1872-1879
Common in Aqua
Rare in Colors
Varient: Codd Type and Hutch
Locale: Sacramento, Cal.
Note: This bottle is common up and down the Central Valley, and the Gold Country. They have also been found in Benicia and as far west as Marin Co.

HISTORY: The first listing of E.L. Billings in the soda or mineral water business was in 1857. He was listed as Billings & Casey, Soda Factory, Alley near the Dawson House. He remained in the mineral water and wholesale liquor business until he died in 1883. The only exception were the years of 1859-1865. When he was listed as a liquor merchant in Folsom with William Timson as a partner in the business.

1853-1854 Billings & Sawyer, Liquor Merchants, Front between M & N Sts.
1854-1855 Billings & Thomas, Bottlers, Front between M & N Sts.
1856   No Listing
1857-1858 Billings & Casey, Soda Factory, Alley near Dawson House
1859-1865 Wm. Timson & E.L. Billings, wholesale dealers in fine wines, liquors and cigars. California Port Wine for sale by Timson & Billings, agent for Hunter's California Wheat Whiskey, pure cognac, brandies and Rochelle Brandy, Leidesdorff St. opposite the freight station, Folsom Cal.
1866-1867 E.L. Billings, Union Soda Works, 49 Front St.
1868-1869 E.L. Billings, wholesale liquor dealers and soda manufacturers, 111 K St.
1872-1879 E.L. Billings & Co., wholesale dealers in in fine brandies and liquors, also for natural soda water from the Geyser Springs, Sonoma County, 111 K St., between 4th and 5th
1879-1880 E.L. Billings & Co., Importers and dealers of fine brandies, wine and liquors. Agents for Jaffe's Celebrated Cinchona Bitters and agents for Lytton Springs Seltzer Water, Sonoma County, Ca., 111 K St.
1880-1884 E.L. Billings & Co., (James Woodburn), wholesale and retail liquor dealers, 417 K St.

The bottle above was in use from 1872-1879, when he was an agent for Geyser Soda. He also had the words "SPARKLING MEAD" trade marked in 1870. See below. The ad is from 1867, showing Billings' liquor business was still going strong.

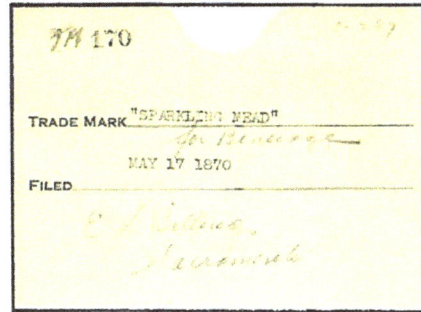

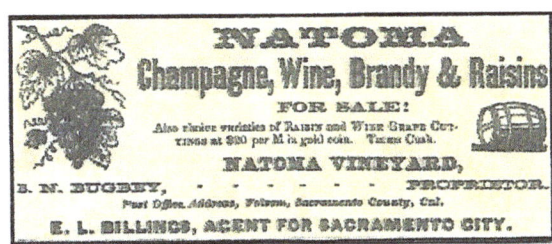

Front: B & G / SAN FRANCISCO
Re: SUPERIOR / MINERAL WATER

Round, 10 Sided Mug Base, Iron Pontil
Applied Top
Cobalt, $475.00 - 2021
Green, $675.00 - 1995
Aqua, $4400.00 - 2017
Benicia Effect, $750.00 - 2019
Scarce in Cobalt
Ex. Rare in other Colors
Circa: 1852-1856
Locale: San Francisco
Note: Normally found in any pontil era town, and the Gold Country. The Forest Hill area in Placer Co. yielded several. Many came out of the mud flats around Benicia and in the Benicia Arsenal. The author has personally dug 7 in privys in Benicia.

HISTORY: 1852 Bache & Grotjan, Wholesale and Retail Druggists and Apothecaries, Washington St. and Plaza
1854-1853 Bache & Grotjan, Druggist 213 Washington
1854-1855 Grotjan & Company, Druggist, 213 Washington
1856 Grotjan & Company, Drug Brokers, 112 California
Ad below is from 1852.

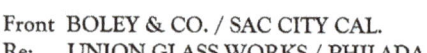

Front BOLEY & CO. / SAC CITY CAL.
Re: UNION GLASS WORKS / PHILADA.

Round, Open and Iron Pontil
Applied Top
Cobalt, $500.00 - 2021, $325.00 - 2021
Varient: reverse is blank, $325.00 - 2018
Variant: reverse has blank plate, $900.00 - 2021
Scarce with Iron Pontil
Ex. Rare with Open Pontil
Variant: "CAL" is embossed in a different way
Circa: 1850-1862
Locale: Sacramento, Cal.
Note: Boley's have been found in many Gold Rush settlements as well as Sacramento. Early Sierra Co. gold camps Monte Cristo and Excelsior yielded this bottle. A few have have been dug in Nevada City.

HISTORY: In late 1849 Addison and Lafayette Boley established the first soda water business in Sacramento, with a capacity bottling five hundred dozen bottles per day. The factory was first located on Front St. between H & I, and remained at this location until 1853. In 1853 Boley & Co. were located on Front St. above the slough. The years of 1854-55 found Boley located on the levee above the Water Works. In 1856 they moved back to Front St., where they remained until 1862. After 1862 Boley & Co. were no longer listed in any businesses in Sacramento.

Front: H. BRADER & CO. / PENALTY / FOR SELLING / THIS BOTTLE / XLCR / SODA WORKS / 738 BROADWAY / S.F.

8 Sided, Smooth Base
Applied Top
Aqua, $1700.00 - 2017 (bruise)
Ex. Rare
Circa: 1863-1864
Locale: San Francisco
Note: This bottle has been found mostly in the San Francisco area, with one coming out of the early port town of Suisun City in Solano. Co.

HISTORY: Christian, Henry, Peter and Louis Brader were in the soda water business in S.F. for over 10 years. And also in Marysville for a few years, 1858-1859.
1862-1864 Brader & Co. (Wm. Hartman), Excelsior Soda Factory, 738 Broadway.
These are the only years they are listed as H. Brader & Co.

Front: "FISH" / BREIG & SCHAFER / S.F.

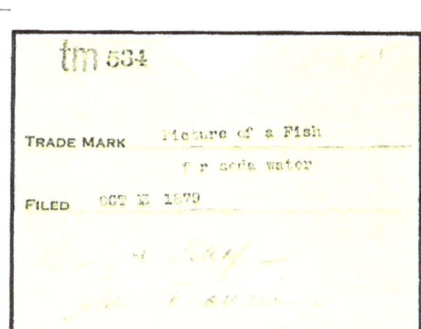

Round, Smooth Base
Applied and Tooled Top
Aqua, A.T., $190.00 - 2021
Green Aqua, A.T. $110.00 - 2019
Scarce
Varient: Hutch
Circa: 1879 - 1890
Locale: San Francisco

HISTORY: John Breig and George Schafer were the proprietors of the Pacific Soda Works from 1879 to 1890. From 1879 thru 1886 their works were located at 38 Hayes, and from 1887 to 1890 at 1710-1712 Folsom. In 1890 and 1891 Breig and Gustavus Bauer were listed as being the proprietors of the Pacific Soda Works, and from 1892 till 1899 Breig and Charles Schafer were listed as the proprietors, still at 1710-171 Folsom. They trade marked the "FISH" logo for soda water in 1879. See above.

Front: BREMENKAMPF & REGLI / EUREKA / NEV.

Round, Smooth Base
Applied and Tooled Top
Aqua, $425.00 - 2010
Aqua, Tooled Top, $925.00 - 2021
Lime Green, $850.00 - 2009, $250.00 - 2021
Common in Aqua
Rare in Green
Circa: 1877-1882
Locale: Eureka, Nevada

HISTORY: In the 1870's Edward Bremenkampf and Joseph Regli were the proprietors of a brewery on Main St. In 1878 they apparently expanded their business to include soda water and liquors. This business remained until 1886, at which time they were no longer listed in the soda water business. They were probably the first soda works in Eureka.

Front: W.H. BURT / SAN FRANCISCO

Round, Iron Pontil
Applied Top
Green, $475.00 - 2021
Benicia Effect, $950.00 - 2019
Scarce
Circa: 1852
Locale: San Francisco
Note: Commonly found in San Francisco redevelopment areas, the mud flats around Benicia and Gold Rush era mining camps. One was dug at the site of Eureka in Sierra Co. and at the Golden Bear Mine in Sierra Co.

HISTORY: In 1851 the soda water business of Cammet & Buffum on Spofford St. was sold to William H. Burt. He ran the business until the end of 1852 and then returned to Pittsburgh Pa.

Front: CALIFORNIA / SELTZER WATER
Re: 'BEAR' / B & G

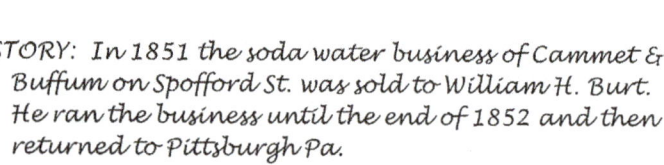

Round Quart, Smooth Base
Applied Top
Aqua, $8500.00 - 2008
Ex. Rare
Circa: 1875-1885
Locale: San Francisco

HISTORY: Like the 'H' in H & G nothing is known about the 'B' on this bottle. See next bottle.

Front: CALIFORNIA / NATURAL / SELTZER WATER
Re: 'BEAR' / H & G

Round, Smooth Base
Applied Top
Cobalt, $16,000.00 - 2015
Lime Green, $4600.00 - 2007
Aqua, $650.00 - 2021
Scarce in Aqua
Ex. Rare in Colors
Varient: Grass under Bear
Circa: 1875-1885
Locale: San Francisco
Note: 2 aqua specimens have come out of Santa Rosa in Sonoma Co. A cobalt one was dug in Carson City, Nevada.

HISTORY: The California Seltzer Springs was located 12 miles from Cloverdale in Sonoma County. There is not much info on this bottle or its quart size brother. No info at all on the H of "H & G". We do know that the G stood for William Garrett, who was the owner of th springs. He applied for a trade mark in 1875, see drawing above. J. Malan was the agent from 1875 to the mid 1880's, with his business being located at 513 Market St. S.F.

Front: CALIFORNIA SODA WORKS / H. FICKEN / S.F.
Re: "EAGLE"

Round, Smooth Base
Applied Top
Aqua, $190.00 - 2019
Lime Green, $1900.00 - 2017, $950.00 - 2021
Green, $3000.00 - 2019
Rare
Circa: 1878-79
Locale: San Francisco
Note: This bottle is usually found in the San Francisco bay area, with specimens coming out of Benicia, Vallejo, Napa and Suisun. San Diego is the furthest away that one has been found.

HISTORY: Henry Ficken is listed as being the proprietor of California Soda Works in 1878-79 and a driver for the Eureka Soda Works in 1880-81. These were both at 723 Turk St. S.F.

Front: OWEN CASEY / EAGLE SODA / WORKS
Re: SAC CITY

Round, Smooth Base
Applied Top
Green, $1000.00 - 2009, $550.00 - 2021
Cobalt, $275.00 - 2021
Lime Green, $600.00 - 2007
Aqua, $180.00 - 2021
Dark Cobalt, $350.00 - 2019
Common in Shades of Blue and Aqua
Rare in Greens
Varient: Hutch
Circa: 1867-1871
Locale: Sacramento
Note: These are found in just about all towns with water access. Mining camps in Sierra Co. have produced a few.

HISTORY: Hugh Casey was in partnership with Michael Cronan starting in 1875, when Casey's former partner Hugh Kelly died. They were listed at 50 K St. in Sacramento until 1886 when Cronan left to form his own business venture. Hugh Casey continued as the proprietor of the Eagle Soda Works until 1905. Ad from the Sacramento business directory circa 1876.

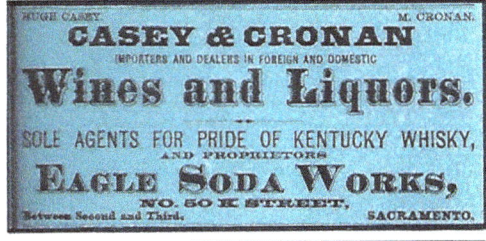

Front: CASSIN'S / ENGLISH / AERATED / WATERS

Round Bottom Soda, Smooth Base
Applied Top
Aqua
Teal Green, $2400.00 - 2021
Rare
Circa: 1872
Locale: San Francisco

HISTORY: The Cassin Bros. tried their hand in the soda water business in 1872. It was not a success as these bottles are very rare. Ad above was placed in the San Francisco Cronicle on April 2, 1872

Front: C C & B / SAN FRANCISCO
Re: SUPERIOR / MINERAL WATER

Round, 10 Sided Mug Base, Iron Pontil
Applied Top
Cobalt, $12,500.00 - 1996, $14,000.00 - 2015
Ex. Rare
Circa: 1856-1857
Locale: San Francisco
Note: Only 2 recent finds of this rare bottle have come to my attention. One was found in the Napa River during some redevelopment in downtown Napa, in 2009, and another was dug in the early town of Alvarado in the East Bay, this was in 2014 or 2015. At least 4 examples were found in the Georgetown, Cal. area in the early 1980's.

HISTORY: Crowell, Crane & Brigham were in business less than 2 years. They were not listed in the 1858 directory and probably went out of business sometime in 1857. Located at 131 Commercial St., two doors down from Montgomery. This bottle appears to have been blown into an altered B & G mold. Almost all mug base sodas have the Union Glass Works marking on the reverse. To my knowledge all of the mug base sodas were blown at the Union Glass Works in Philadelphia. The B & G and the C C & B are the only two that do not have the Glass Works markings on the reverse. Both ads below are circa 1856. Early box from the Max Bell collection.

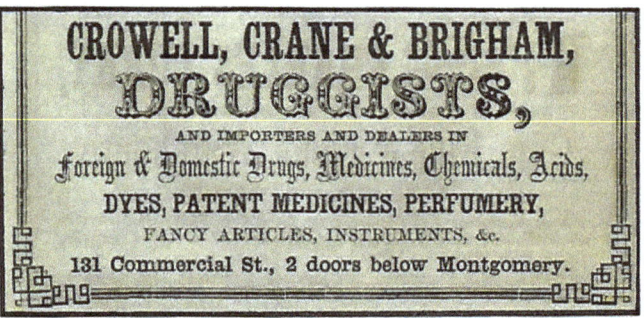

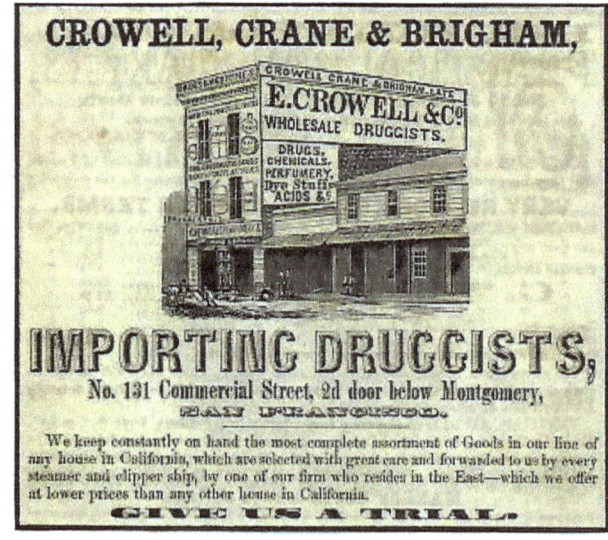

Front: CHASE & CO. / MINERAL WATER / SAN FRANCISCO / STOCKTON & / MARYSVILLE / CAL

Round, Iron Pontil
Applied Top
Green, $1300.00 - 2017
Rare
Circa: 1853-1854
Note: Ad circa 1853.

HISTORY: By Aug. 9th, 1853 Frederick C. Chase is in partnership with William C. Westgate, William C. Pease & A.W. Cudworth. April 1st, 1854, the "copartnership existing under the name and style of CHASE & CO. in San Francisco, Stockton and Marysville, Soda Water Manufacturers is this day dissolved by mutual consent."

Stockton:
1853-54 Chase & Co., Common & Market Sts.
1854-55 Chase & Co., Soda Factory corner Market and Commerce Sts.

Chase & Co. was the first soda water manufactory in Stockton. A.D. Vaughn took over the business in 1856.

Marysville:
1853-54 Chase & Co. Soda Manufactory, NE Corner 6th and alley above A St.
1854-55 Chase & Co., Soda Factory, corner 6th and A St.

Front: CHASE & CO. / MINERAL WATER / SAN FRANCISCO / CAL. (in slug plate)

Round, Iron Pontil
Applied Top
Green, $250.00 - 2017
Scarce
Circa: 1852-1854
Locale: San Francisco
Note: Ad at right circa 1854. Both versions of the Chase bottle come out of the S.F. redevelopment areas, the Benicia mud flats, Benicia Arsenal, and in Sierra Co. mining camps of Mountain House and Monte Cristo.

History: January 22nd, 1852 Jorgensen & Chase partnership dissolved in San Francisco. Feb. 16, 1852 Chase & Co. successor to Lynde & Putnam mineral water manufactory, now located at Broadway near Kearny Sts. San Francisco.
1853 Chase & Co., Soda Water Manufactory, Broadway near Kearny
1854 Chase & Co., Soda Factory, Vallejo, Hinckley & Pinckney Sts.
1854-1855 Cudworth, A.W., firm of Chase & Co. / cor., Vallejo and Pinckney
In 1856 Cudworth assumed ownership of Chase & Co., which was established in 1851 on Kearny St. and moved to the corner of Hinckley and Pinckney Sts. in 1853.

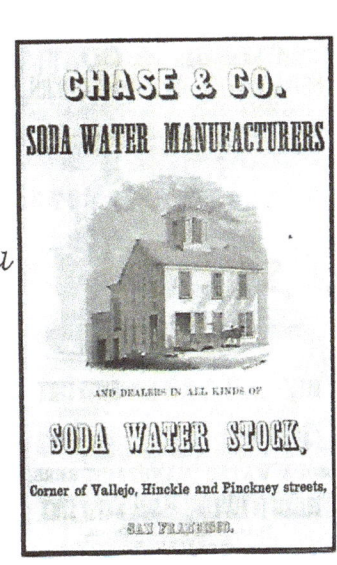

Front: CHAMPAGNE / MEAD

8 Sided, Smooth Base
Applied Top
Aqua, $70.00 - 2019
Deep Lime Green, $500.00 - 2013 (bruise)
Common in Aqua
Rare in Colors
Circa: 1871-72
Locale: San Francisco
Note: Although this company was not in business very long, their bottles are not rare. They seem to be all over Northern California, with many coming out of Sacramento, Pittsburg, and Antioch area.

HISTORY: There are two patents for this product that are somewhat confusing. Seems that Frank Kenyon & Co. of San Francisco, patented the name "CHAMPAGNE MEAD" on April 5, 1870 in California. Then on August 16, 1870, Asher S. Taylor patented with the U.S. Patent Office, what he called and "improved beverage called Champagne Mead". This is the same Asher Taylor that had a pontiled soda with his name on it in the 1850's.

A small article in the Sacramento Daily Union on April 6, 1870, states that Frank Kenyon & Co. trade marked the name "Champagne Mead". See below. The only listing found for San Francisco is as follows: 1871-1872 Gass & Co., William C. Gass, John Boland & W.H. Emerson, Champagne Mead Works at 114 Turk St. S.F.

On May 27, 1870, the Sacramento Daily Union ran an ad listing Thos. Davidson, agent at 134 K St., Sacramento. See below. On August 20, 1870 a dissolution notice was filed between Frank Kenyon, W.C. Gass and W. Fowler. This was four days after Taylor applied for his patent. See below. At this point the company seemed to be out of business.

Front: C & K / EAGLE WORKS / SAC CITY

Round, Smooth Base
Applied Top
Cobalt, $300.00 - 2021
Common
Circa: 1858-1866
Locale: Sacramento
Note: Casey and Kelly were in Virginia City from 1862-1866 according to Holabird. Virginia City ad is from 1866. Sacramento ad circa 1862. They applied for a trade mark for painted marks on their bottles in 1861 and the "C & K" name in 1863. Many of these bottles have been dug in the Sacramento area and in Virginia City.

HISTORY: 1858-1860 Casey & Kelly, importers and dealers in liquors, wines, brandies, wholesale and retail Soda Bottling Establishment, 109 K St. between 4th & 5th

1860-1866 Casey & Kelly, Soda Factory, 107 K St. between 4th & 5th

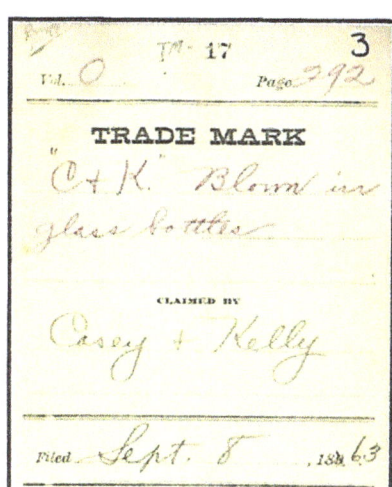
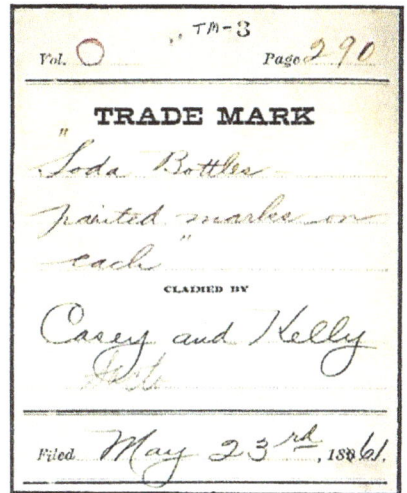

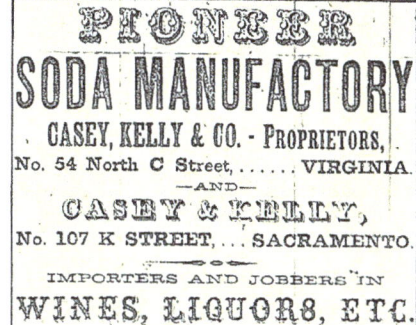

Front: CLASSEN & CO. / SAN / FRANCISCO
Re: PACIFIC / SODA / WORKS

Round, Smooth Base
Applied Top
Deep Aqua, $100.00 - 2019
Teal Blue, $400.00 - 2021
Aqua, $100.00 - 2021
Lt. Green, $130.00 - 2021
Common
Varient: Has a different font and the embossing is lower on the body.
  Teal Green, $750.00 - 2017, Rare
Circa: 1863-1868
Locale: San Francisco
Note: In 1863, Classen trade marked the name and embossing pattern. Commonly found in the San Francisco bay area and in Benicia, Vallejo and Antioch.

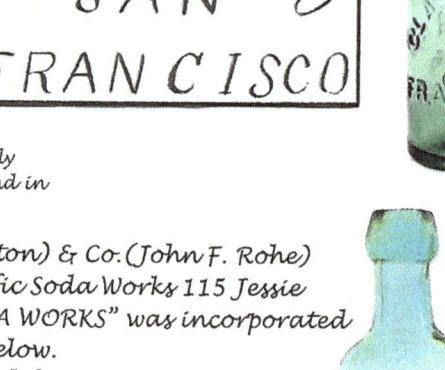

HISTORY: 1863-1867 Classen (J. Milton) & Co. (John F. Rohe) Proprietors Pacific Soda Works 115 Jessie
The "SAN FRANCISCO PACIFIC SODA WORKS" was incorporated on Jan. 31, 1863, See certificate below.
On April 25, 1867 the Daily Alta California ran a notice of dissolution between partners Classen and Rohe. John Rohe continued as proprietor until 1871 when he went to work at the Bay City Soda Water Co. J. Milton Classen retired.

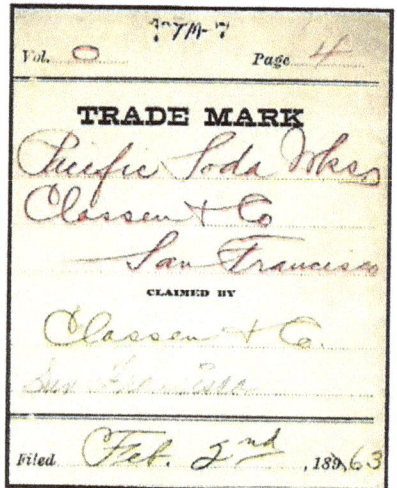

16

Front: CLASSEN & CO. / "ANCHORS" / SPARKLING (on shoulder)

    Round, Smooth Base
    Applied Square Top
    Cobalt, $375.00 - 2021
    Teal Green, $100.00 - 2007 (chips)
    Deep Aqua, $275.00 - 2021
    Scarce
    Circa: 1864-1868
    Locale: San Francisco
    Note: This bottle held "Anchor Brand Sparkling Cider", which was manufactured and sold by Classen & Co. 1864-1868. These bottles were once considered very rare, but the "BIG DIG" in San Francisco in 1998, yielded many more. This was the site of a used bottle dealer and contained many specimens of rare western blown bottles.

HISTORY: See Classen & Co. (previous bottle)

Front: COLUMBIA / NAPA / TRADE "EAGLE" MARK / COUNTY / MINERAL WATER

    Round, Smooth Base
    Tooled Top
    Aqua
    Ex. Rare
    Circa: 1892-1894*
    Locale: San Francisco

HISTORY: * Since there is no info on this bottle and from the way it is embossed we are going to do some assuming. The embossing " Napa Trade Mark County" is the same as the embossing on the Walters Napa bottle, except this one has an Eagle the Walters has a horseshoe. There were no Columbia Springs in Napa Co, which makes us believe that the water in this bottle was actually from the Walters Springs. It was being sold by G.L. Abell, who was the sole agent for Walters Springs from 1892 to 1894. The listing for Abell was: Walters Napa Soda, the leading mineral water. Depot 641 Mission, G.L. Abell, sole agent.

Front: COLUMBIA / SODA / WORKS / S.F.
Re: "SEATED LIBERTY" / C.C. DALL

    Round, Smooth Base
    Applied Top
    Lt. Green, $3800.00 - 2017
    Deep Aqua, $400.00 - 2011
    Aqua, $400.00 - 2021
    Scarce in Aqua
    Ex. Rare in Amber
    Rare in Green
    Circa: 1878-1881
    Locale: San Francisco and Oakland

HISTORY: 1878-1879 Columbia Soda Works, Christopher Dall proprietor, 733 Broadway S.F.
    1880-1881 Dall, Christopher, Proprietor Columbia Soda Works, Oakland

Mr. Dall once worked at the U.S. Mint, where he no doubt got the idea for the Seated Liberty on his bottles. There were coins with the same pattern embossed on them. The reason he moved to Oakland is unknown at this time. He was no longer listed in the soda water trade after 1881.

Front: CONNOLLY & BRO. / S.F.
Re: GEYSER SODA

Round, Smooth Base
Applied Top
Aqua
Green
Cobalt, $2700.00 - 2008
Rare in Aqua
Ex. Rare in Blue and Green
Varient: minus "S.F.", Common
          Aqua, $60.00 - 2021
Circa: 1862-1868
Locale: San Francisco
Note: Ad at right circa 1867. The Connolly Bro's trade marked the Geyser Soda name in 1867. See crude drawing below. Numerous specimens without the "S.F." have been found in Marin Co., and a cobalt example was dug in Suisun City in 1978. They have also been found in Sacramento.

HISTORY: 1862-1868, Connolly Bros., Geyser Soda office, 722 Front St. S.F. After 1868 they were no longer listed in the soda or mineral water business in S.F. Bottles without the S.F. embossing may have been used by the Connolly's in Petaluma, where from 1872 thru 1876 they were listed as manufacturers and bottlers of ale, porter, soda water, etc. The bottles without "S.F." would then date from 1872-1876. After 1876 the company was known as B.F. Connolly & Co. and was an agent for Napa Soda.

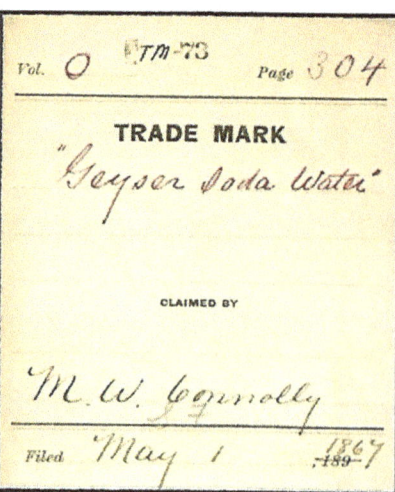

Front: "CROSS"
Re: "CROSS"

    Round, Iron Pontil
    Applied Top
    Green, $3200.00 - 2021
    Rare
    Circa: 1850's
    Locale: Unknown

HISTORY: These bottles are eastern blown but most known specimens have been dug in the West. The Georgetown, Cal. area in the Gold Country is where most of these have been found.

Front: COTTLE, POST & CO. / "EAGLE" / PORTLAND OGN

    Round, Smooth Base
    Tooled Top
    Teal Blue
    Amber, $1800.00 - 2007
    Teal Green, $950.00 - 2021
    Rare in Green
    Ex. Rare in Amber
    Circa: 1877-1881
    Locale: Portland, Oregon

HISTORY: The Cottle & Post company was first listed in the soda business in 1877. They were located at 146 Front St in Portland until 1881. No further listing of them together in the soda business.

Front: C & R / EAGLE WORKS / SAC CITY

    Round, Smooth Base
    Applied Top
    Cobalt, $1400.00 - 2021
    Ex. Rare
    Circa: 1860
    Locale: Sacramento

HISTORY: In 1860 a James Kelly was listed at the business of C & R, located at 109 K St. This was also the location of the C & K Eagle Soda Works. It is believed that James Kelly was using the reputation of Casey & Kelly to help sell his product. In 1861 Casey & Kelly applied for a trade mark and moved their soda water business to 107 K St. After 1861 there is no further mention of the James Kelly fellow.

Front: CRYSTAL / S.W. CO. / S.F. / CIDER
Base: "TRIANGLE"

Round, Smooth Base
Applied Top
Amber, $8000.00 - 2019 (potstone)
$2800.00 - 2021 (bruise)
Ex. Rare
Circa: 1886
Locale: San Francisco
Note: One whole specimen was dug in Oakland.

HISTORY: In 1886 The Crystal Soda Water Co. applied for a trade mark on this bottle. The cider market must have been slow and it was discontinued shortly after 1886. See drawing.

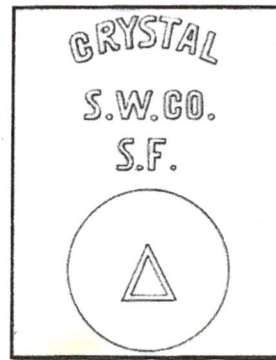

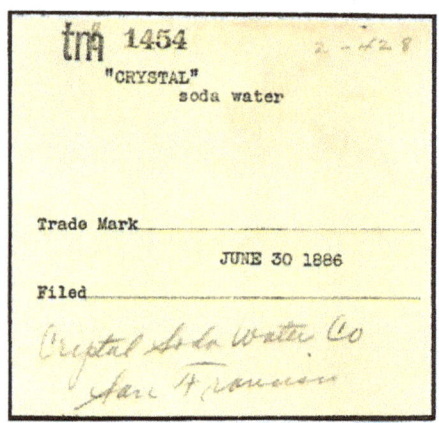

Front: CRYSTAL / SODA / WATER
Re: PATENTED / NOV. 12-1872 / TAYLOR'S / U.S. PT.

Round, Smooth Footed Base
Applied Blob and Collared Top
Cobalt, Blob Top, $1100.00 - 2017
Aqua, Collar Top, $110.00 - 2021
Deep Teal Green, $1600.00 - 2007
Cobalt, Collar Top, $250.00 - 2021
Variant: without "TAYLOR'S / U.S. PT."
  Cobalt, Collar Top, $275.00 - 2010
  Aqua, Collar Top, $210.00 - 2017
  Cobalt, Blob Top, $700.00 - 2019
  Lt. Blue, Blob Top, $350.00 - 2021
Variant: Top has a pinhole.
     Hutch Style Bottle
Common with Collar Top
Scarce with Blob Top
Ex. Rare in Green
Circa: 1873-1889
Locale: San Francisco
Note: Ad above right is circa: 1874.
   These sodas are found all over the bay area,
   concentrated in the Antioch, Pittsburg area.

HISTORY: Sylvester Simmons and Frank Maxon were involved with this company in various positions from 1873-1889. They were either president, superintendent, or secretary at different times. The Crystal Soda Water Co. was incorporated on August 8, 1873, with the trustees being Frederick Clay, Adolph Weske, John Meaburn, Asher Taylor, Noah Miles and Gilbert Dean. Seems that Asher Taylor had his hands in many different soda companys.

Front: A.W. CUDWORTH / & CO / SAN FRANCISCO / CAL. (in slug plate)
       A.W. CUDWORTH / & CO / SAN FRANCISCO (in slug plate)
       A.W. CUDWORTH / SAN FRANCISCO (in slug plate)

Round, Iron Pontil and Smooth Base
Applied Top
Green, Iron Pontil, $500.00 - 2021
Aqua, Smooth Base, $150.00 - 2009
Greenish Aqua, $600.00 - 2021
Benicia Effect, Iron Pontil, $600.00 - 2019
Common in Aqua
Scarce in Green
Varient: Different Size Font
Circa: 1856-1861
Locale: San Francisco
Note: bottles without "& CO." circa 1859-61
These bottles have been found in the S.F. redevelopment areas, and in Benicia, at the mud flats and Benicia Arsenal. They are also found at numerous early Gold Rush camps including Eureka and Chaparral Hill in Sierra Co. Forest Hill in Placer Co. produced several.

HISTORY: This company was previously known as Chase & Co.
- 1856 - Eagle, Cudworth & Co., corner Hinckley, Pinckney and Vallejo Sts.
- 1857 - A.W. Cudworth, dwl corner of Hinckley and Pinckney Place
- 1858 - Cudworth & Co. (W.C. Pease), proprietors of the Excelsior Soda Factory, corner Hinckley and Pinckney
- 1859-1860 - Cudworth, A.W., Soda Manufactory, Vallejo between Dupont and Kearney
- 1861 - No mention of Cudworth, shows Brader & Co. as owners of the Excelsior Soda Works

In 1862 Able W. Cudworth entered into the business of importing soda water stock. This lasted one year and he was not listed in any business again until 1875, at which time he was listed as a capitalist and being in the real estate business.

Front: JAMES DASCOMBE / DENVER / COLO.
Re: THIS BOTTLE / IS NEVER SOLD

Round, Smooth Base
Applied Top
Aqua
Ex. Rare
Variant: Hutch
Circa: 1879-1885
Locale: Denver, Colorado

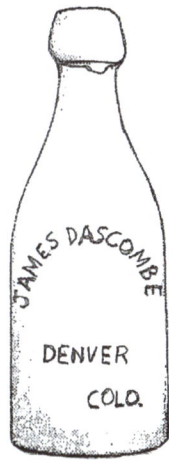

HISTORY: James Dascombe bottled soda water in Denver from the late 1870's until the mid 1880's, at which time a Mr. Schause joined the firm. His address when this bottle was in use was at 328 Holiday St. in Denver.

Front: J. DAY / & CO.

Round, Smooth Base
Applied Top
Aqua, $1100.00 - 2019
Shades of Blue
Rare in Aqua
Ex. Rare in Blue
Circa: 1870's
Locale: Salt Lake City, Utah

HISTORY: No info at this time. This is a territorial bottle as Utah did not become a state until 1896. This bottle has the appearance of a bottle blown in San Francisco.

Front: H. DENHALTER / SALT LAKE CITY / UTAH
Re: A & D.H.C.

Round, Smooth Base
Applied Top
Aqua
Rare
Circa: Early 1880's
Locale: Salt Lake City, Utah

HISTORY: See below.

Front: H. DENHALTER & CO. / SALT LAKE CITY / UTAH
Re: McC

Round, Smooth Base
Applied Top
Aqua
Rare
Circa: 1883-1886
Locale: Salt Lake City, Utah

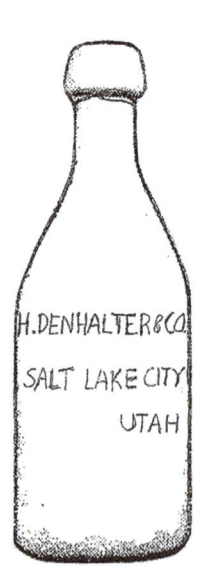

HISTORY: 1882 - Denhalter, Henry & Son, Soda Water Manufacturers,
            123 Commercial, SLC
         1883-84 - Denhalter, H. & H.C., 123 Commercial SLC
            Denhalter, H., Son & Co.(Wm. Lesher), Soda Factory
            123 Commercial SLC
         1886-87 - Denhalter, H. & Son, manufacturers of soda water
            SLC,
         No further listing. These should be considered a territorial bottle as Utah did not become a state intil 1896.

Front: DEAMER / GRASS VALLEY
Re: W.E.D.

Round, Smooth Base
Applied Top
Aqua, $200.00 - 2021
Scarce
Varient: Gravitator
Circa: 1870's to mid 1880's'
Locale: Grass Valley, Ca.
Note: Deamer bottles are found all over the Northern Mines area of California, and down to Marysville and Sacramento. One was dug as far away as Vallejo. They are most common in the Grass Valley and Dutch Flat areas.

HISTORY: W.E. Deamer arrived in San Francisco in 1851. He then moved to Auburn and in 1854 to Nevada City, where he was in the soda water business. He sold out two months later and moved back to Auburn, and then to Europe. He returned to California in 1855, settling in Oroville. Then in 1856 he moved to Grass Valley. In the 1860's he was the proprietor of the Snug Saloon. In the 1870's and 1880's he was the manufacturer of ginger ale, soda water and cider, doing business at the corner of School and Richardson St. He lived on Bean St. Litho below is from the 1880 Nevada County Atlas.

SODA WORKS & RESIDENCE OF W.E. DEAMER,

New discovery

Face: BORDWELL & Co./MINERAL & WATER
Reverse: BORDWELL & Co./MINERAL & WATER

The U.S. census of 1852 shows a John Bordwell of Placer County. Two Bordwell & Co. sodas were dug in Auburn under the old Shanghai Bar and Restaurant about 20 years ago. The building dates to the Gold Rush. There is evidence of a Bordwell in the soda business in Oroville in 1857 and 1858 with W. E. Deamer. Other research shows Bordwell associated with the soda business in Gold Rush area towns. Strong evidence leads us to believe this is a Western soda.

Bottle image from Mike Southworth's collection
Addendum 23-A

Revelations of a Horse Thief
Rattlesnake Dick

A person named Win. Sheridan, says The Oroville Record in the Court of Sessions, on Thursday, plead guilty to the charge of grand larceny. He stole a horse from Messrs. Deamer & **Bordwell,** of that place in December last, and was traced to Grass Valley, Nevada county, where he was arrested by Deputy Sherriff McLaughlin, and brought back.

He was induced to take the horse from hero by one Charley Hardy, who pointed out the house and barn, and stood guard for him, he never having seen the place until it was shown him by Hardy.

Hardy was to meet him at Placerville with another horse, when they intended going to Salt Lake, and from thence to the Atlantic States in the coming spring. He came to California in 1848, in Company F. Third Artillery, and after his discharge, served as a volunteer, in Captain Bowlin's Co. during the Indian troubles of '51, Followed mining until '64, when he was arrested for grand larceny, at Mokelumne Hill, Calaveras county, and sentenced to State Prison for a term of two years, eighteen months of which he served out, and then effected his escape while (the Prison was under the management of Estell, then when it was under the management of the State Directors, and that the prisoners had better fare,

After his escape, he went south, and at Sonora, became associated with a gang of horse thieves. There was also an organized band of horse thieves at Grass Valley, which has been broken up by the arrest of Jim Webster, now in the Marysville jail. Webster had just been convicted of grand larceny in Yuba County. Sheridan says Webster is an escaped convict, and was known in prison as Rattlesnake Dick. This organized band of horse thieves extends throughout the State, with agencies for selling stolen horses at Jackson, Sonora and Shasta.

Tom Edwards was their agent in Sonora, and Jack Hoyle in Jackson. He was unacquainted with the agent's name in Shasta as he had never been at that place; but says that Frank Stone and Hob O'Neil, of Shasta are connected with the band. He says there are more thieves at the present time in the State than ever, and that nearly every town contains an organized band. He states that there is an establishment near Auburn, Placer County, where counterfeit coin is manufactured, and which he assures us was exceedingly well executed and calculated to deceive the most experienced money changers. When he first came to Oroville, he recognized about fifty old offenders, with whom he was formerly acquainted. He says they extend from Oroville, to Spanish town and Wyandotte. When he entered Smith's gambling house in Oroville, and glanced at the crowd there assembled, he really considered himself in the "den of forty thieves." They have congregated here from every portion of the State. Sometime in December, a plan was laid by these scoundrels, to fire Oroville and plunder the town, but that it was postponed until next spring, when the miners would be at work in the immediate vicinity, and money much more plenty, He was so in formed by a person called "Dublin Jack."

Placer Herald - February 21, 1857

Addendum 23-B

Front: D.S. & CO. / SAN FRANCISCO (in slug plate)

Round, Smooth Base
Applied Top
Green
Aqua, $325.00 - 2021
Cobalt, $1100.00 - 2021
Deep Prussian Blue, $2800.00 - 2017
Scarce in Aqua
Rare in Green and Blue
Ex. Rare in Prussian Blue
Circa: 1861-1864
Locale: San Francisco
Note: Delahanty & Skelly trade marked the name in 1861. See crude drawing below. Ad below right circa 1862. A cobalt one was dug in Grass Valley in the early 1980's but most come out of the San Francisco Bay area.

HISTORY: 1854-1859 Delahanty & Skelly, Empire Soda Works, Mission near Third
1860- Skelly & Co., Proprietors, Empire Soda Works, E Side Third between Jessie and Stevensen
1861-1864 Delahanty, Skelly & Co., proprietors Empire Soda Works, 29 Third.
This is the first year the company is listed as D.S. & Co.

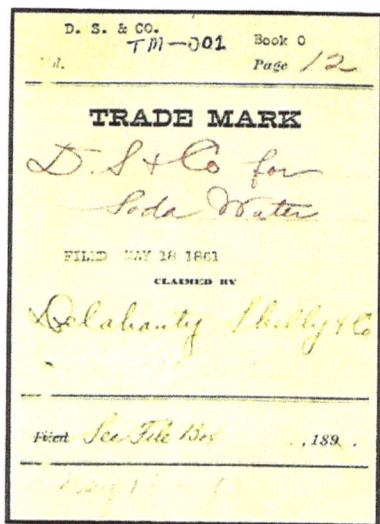

Front: DITZ & ELLERKAMP / SAN FRANCISCO / SODA WORKS

Round, Smooth Base
Applied Top
Aqua
Ex. Rare
Circa: 1868-1872
Locale: San Francisco
Note: This is one of the rarest Western Sodas.

HISTORY: 1868-1870 Ellerkamp (Benjamin) & Co. (N. Gerdes) and Andrew Ditz, proprietors San Francisco Soda Works, Hinckley nr Dupont
1871-1872 Ellerkamp & Co. proprietors San Francisco Soda Works, 22 Hinckley
1872-1873 Ditz, Andrew soda bottler, dwl 415 ½ Clementina
No further listings for Gerdes or Ellerkamp
Ellerkamp next shows up as a driver for the Bay City Soda Water Co. in 1873
1873 John N. Gerdes now listed as the proprietor of the San Francisco Soda Works, 22 Hinckley

Front: "EAGLE" (in slug plate)

Round, Open and Iron Pontil
Applied Top
Teal Green, I.P., $230.00 - 2008 (slug plate)
Green, I.P., $500.00 - 2021 (slug plate)
Green, I.P., $200.00 - 2018 (non slug)
Benicia Effect, I.P., $700.00 - 2019 (slug plate)
Common with Iron Pontil
Ex. Rare with Open Pontil
Circa: 1852-1862
Locale: Sacramento
Note: This bottle is found thru out the Gold Country and many early towns along the Sacramento and San Joaquin rivers. Auburn and Nevada City have produced several. Dozens have come out of the Benicia mud flats, and in pontil era privys in Benicia. These were no doubt on boats coming west from Sacramento.

HISTORY: There is not enough info to establish a for sure location for this bottle. We are going to guess and say its the forerunner of the C & K Eagle works bottle. The majority of known specimens have been found in and around Sacramento, Benicia and S.F. I personally have dug 12-15 in Benicia myself. The bottles no doubt found their way down river on excursion boats. Another factor is that Sacramento was the only location where a Eagle Soda Works was listed as being in business during the years the bottle should have been dated from. According to the Thompson & West 1880 history of Sacramento County in 1880 they state " there are in operation now the factory of Casey & Cronan whose place of business is at 218 K St. They were the successors of Casey & Kelly, who commenced in business in 1852." Being that C & K were the proprietors of the Eagle Works, which was embossed on their bottles and they were probably blown at the Pacific Glass Works who started operations in 1863. We feel it is safe to assume that C & K used the pontilled Eagle bottles from 1852 until their factory burned down in 1863. At that point they began using the bottles blown at the Pacific Glass Works.

Front: EASTERN / CIDER CO.

Round, Smooth Base
Applied Top
Dark Amber, $210.00 - 2021
Yellow Amber, $1100.00 - 2019
Olive Green, $7000.00 - 2017
Olive Amber, $1300.00 - 2019
Common in Amber
Rare in Green and Lighter Colors
Varient: Hutch
Circa: 1877-1882
Locale: San Francisco and Oakland
Note: Many have been found in the Oakland and East Bay area over the years. One was dug in Dutch Flat even.

HISTORY: 1877-1880 Eastern Cider Co., Donald Mitchell Superintendent, 719 Bryant S.F.
1880-1881 Blevins, James & Co. proprietors Pioneer Soda Factory and agent for Pacific Congress Water and Eastern Cider, N E cor 13th and Franklin, Oakland
1881-1882 Blevins & Mitchell dealers in Pacific Congress Water, Lytton Springs and P.S. Seltzer Water, agents for Eastern Cider, 29 Montgomery S.F.

Front: EL – DORADO

Round, Smooth Base
Applied Top
Aqua, $90.00 - 2021
Green, $325.00 - 2010
Common
Circa: 1860's
Locale: unknown
Note: This popular bottle has been found all over the Sierra Nevada gold mining regions, as well as in the San Francisco bay area. One was dug in the Wilmington district of Fremont, as well as Concord, Antioch, Martinez and Suisun City. Many have been dug in Nevada City and the Forest Hill area of Placer Co.

HISTORY: There is no diffinitive info on this bottle. They have been dug mostly in the west, so they are no doubt western in origin. Especially with an historic name like EL DORADO.

Front: HENRY H. ELLIS / CHEYENNE / W.T.
Re: H.H.E. (block letters)

Round, Smooth Base
Applied Top
Aqua
Rare
Circa: Mid 1880's
Locale: Cheyenne, Wyoming

HISTORY: Henry Ellis was the proprietor of a bakery and confectionery shop, which was located at 291 Eddy St. (Pioneer St.) from around 1884 to 1887. This is a territory bottle as Wyoming became a state in 1890.

Front: ELLIS & BROTHER / CHEYENNE / W.T.

    Round, Smooth Base
    Applied Top
    Aqua
    Ex. Rare
    Circa: mid 1880's
    Locale: Cheyenne, Wyoming

HISTORY: See previous bottle.

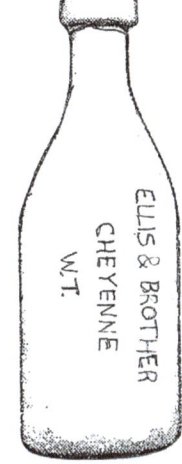

Front: T. EMMETT / OGDEN, UTAH

    Round, Smooth Base
    Applied Top
    Aqua
    Rare
    Varient: Hutch
    Circa: 1880's
    Locale: Ogden, Utah
    Note: Even though these bottles are hard to find in Utah, one made its way out west. It was dug in Marin County, Cal., in the early 2000's.

HISTORY: Throughout the 1880's Thomas Emmett was the proprietor of a soda works on the corner of 7th and Franklin Sts. This is the only blob top soda from Ogden and is a territory bottle as Utah became a state in 1896.

Front: EMPIRE / SODA / WORKS
Re: VALLEJO / E. McG

    Round, Smooth Base
    Applied Top
    Aqua Green
    Ex. Rare
    Circa: 1867-1874
    Locale: Vallejo, Cal.
    Note: Specimens of the bottle have been found in the Solano County towns of Vallejo, Benicia, Vacaville and Suisun City. Napa also yielded one in the late 1990's.

HISTORY: In 1867 Edward McGettigan started the Empire Soda Works in Vallejo on the N.W. corner of Florida and Sonoma Sts. He bottled soda water at that location until 1874. In 1874 McGettigan acquired the soda operation of James McGarvey at the corner of Carolina and Marin Sts. and started the Pioneer Brewery, which he ran until around 1880.

Front: EMPIRE SODA WORKS / SAN FRANCISCO

Round, Smooth Base
Applied Top
Green, $2000.00 - 2019
Cobalt, $800.00 - 2019, 275.00 - 2021
Lime Green, $425.00 - 2021
Blue Green, $750.00 - 2017
Deep Aqua, $190.00 - 2021
Lt. Blue, $190.00 - 2021
Common in Aqua
Rare in Colors
Circa: 1861-1871
Locale: San Francisco
Note: This bottle is found in most Bay Area towns, including Vallejo, Napa, Benicia, Vacaville, Antioch, and San Rafael and Santa Rosa in the North Bay.

HISTORY:
1861-1864 See D.S. & Co. / San Francisco
1864-1865 See Empire Soda Works / D & M
1866-1869 Fagan, Blevins & Co., Empire Soda Works, N.E. corner of Third & Mission
1870-1871 Fagan, Blevins & Co., Empire Soda Works, 353 Third
1871 was the last year Empire Soda Works was listed as being in business until 1880. Then Frank S. Waldo reinstated the name. See next bottle.

Front: EMPIRE SODA WORKS / SAN FRANCISCO
Re: FRANK / S / WALDO

Round, Smooth Base
Applied Top
Aqua, $300.00 - 2017
Rare
Varient: Hutch
Circa: 1880-1882
Locale: San Francisco and Alameda

HISTORY: 1878-79 Waldo, Frank S. (Belfast Ginger Ale Co.) dwl 1717 Market
1880-81 Empire Soda Works, Francis S. Waldo proprietor 1721 Market
1880-81 Waldo, Frank S., Soda Water, ns Eagle Ave Alameda
It seems that Waldo obtained the old Empire molds and put his name on reverse side. He apparently bottled his soda water in Alameda and used the Pioneer Soda Works in S.F. as a distribution point as the address is the same 1721 Market St, in 1880-81.

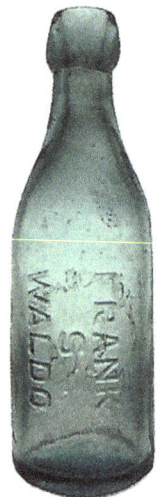

Front: EMPIRE SODA WORKS / D.S. & CO. / SAN FRANCISCO

Round, Smooth Base
Applied Top
Aqua, $650.00 - 2021
Green
Blue
Rare in all Colors
Circa: 1863-1864

HISTORY: See D.S. & Co. / San Francisco.

Front: EMPIRE SODA WORKS / D & M / SAN FRANCISCO

Round, Smooth Base
Applied Top
Cobalt, $550.00 - 2017
Aqua
Green
Scarce in Aqua
Rare in Colors
Circa: 1864-1865
Locale: San Francisco
Note: Name and embossing pattern trade marked in 1864 by Delahanty & McGuirk.

HISTORY: See D.S. & Co.
 1864-65 Delahanty & McGuirk, proprietors Empire Soda Works, 29 Third St.
 1866 No further listing of the partnership of Delahanty & McGuirk

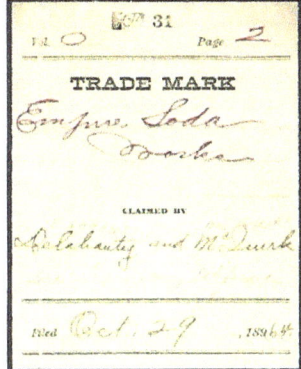
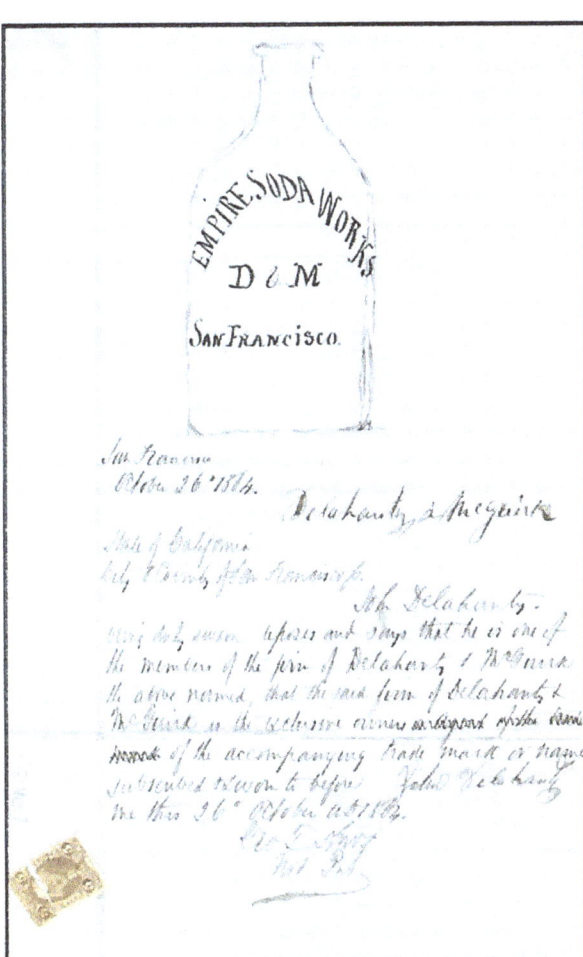

Front: EMPIRE SODA WORKS / VALLEJO
Re: "EAGLE"

Round, Smooth Base
Applied Top
Lt. Green, $350.00 - 2007
Aqua, $275.00 - 2021
Scarce
Varient: Hutch and Crown Top
Circa: 1874-1890
Locale: Vallejo, Cal.
Note: The Vallejo Eagle bottles as they are known locally, are found in greater numbers in neighboring towns than in Vallejo. Specimens have been found in Benicia, Napa, Concord, Martinez and Antioch, with Benicia leading the pack. Most of the bottles that were consumed in Vallejo, must have been returned to the soda factory being the reason for this.

HISTORY: In 1874 Frank and Charles O'Grady were listed as being the proprietors of the Vallejo Empire Soda Works which was located on the corner of Sonoma and Carolina Sts. Around 1878 the O'Gradys relocated to the NW corner of Sonoma and Florida, the location of the original Empire Soda Works, which was started by Edward MCGettigan. After they relocated a F. McDermott joined the firm as a partner, which did not last long, and by the early 1880's Charles O'Grady was no longer listed as being a partner, leaving Frank to run the soda works solo until the early 1890's.

Front: THE / EXCELSIOR / WATER

8 Sided, Iron Pontil
Applied Top
Yellow Green, $550.00 - 2007
Teal Blue, $425.00 - 2021
Deep Em. Green, $300.00 - 2019
Benicia Effect, $600.00 - 2008
Scarce
Varient: "WATER" is slugged in
Circa: 1850's
Locale: San Francisco
Note: This bottle has been found in the Gold Mining districts of Northern California, in the mud flats in Benicia and in the redevelopment areas in San Francisco. One has been dug in San Jose, and one in Suisun City. Nevada City produced one in 1986.

HISTORY: San Francisco was the only town in which we found the business of Excelsior Soda Water listed in the range of years that the bottle should be dated. We feel that this bottle could have been used by one or all of the persons listed below.

1856   Excelsior, corner Jessie & Mission (listed under Soda Water Manufacturers)
1856-1857 Excelsior Soda Factory, Hedley & Co. proprietors, 157 California
1858   A.W. Cudworth & Co., proprietors Excelsior Soda Factory, corner Hinckley and Pinkley
1860-1861 A.W. Cudworth, Excelsior Soda Water Manufacturer, ss Vallejo between Hinckley & Pinkley

Front: EXCELSIOR / SODA / & / MINERAL / WATER / FACTORY

    Round, Smooth Base
    Applied Top
    Aqua, $1300.00 - 2019
    Rare
    Circa: 1875
    Locale: Los Angeles, Cal.
    Note: This bottle is generally found in Southern California with at least 8 coming out of Anaheim. I have not heard of any being found in Northern California.

HISTORY: 1875 Aockerblum, Fritz, proprietor Excelsior Soda and Mineral Water Factory, Round House, Main St.
            Sauer, Louis, Soda Manufacturer, Round House, Main St.

Front: J.A. FARRELL / GRASS VALLEY
Re: F (block letter)

    Round, Smooth Base
    Applied Top
    Aqua, $275.00 - 2021
    Green, Blue
    Scarce in Aqua
    Rare in Colors
    Varient: reverse is blank
    Circa: Late 1860's to 1870's
    Locale: Grass Valley, Cal.
    Note: Commonly found in the Grass Valley, Lowell Hill area.

HISTORY: J.A. Farrell was listed as a Soda Water Manufacturer in the 1860's. No address given. He may have been on Mill St. which in later years had a Soda Water Factory owned by a S.R. Wilder.

Front: F.M. (block letters) / MODESTO

    Round, Smooth Base
    Applied Top
    Aqua, $400.00 - 2021
    Rare
    Circa: 1875-1880
    Locale: Modesto, Cal.

HISTORY: 1875-1880 Meinecke, Frederick, Soda Water Manufacturer, Ninth St. Only listing for this company.

Front: FOUNTAIN & TALLMAN / CALFA
Re: BRIDGETON / N. J.

    Round, Iron Pontil
    Applied Top
    Aqua, $3400.00 - 2015
    Ex. Rare
    Circa: 1853
    Locale: Placerville, Cal.
    Note: Most of the known examples were found in the Georgetown, Cal. area.

HISTORY: In 1853 the soda water factory of John Fountain and Benjamin Tallman was located at what is today 523-525 Main St. At the time Placerville was known as Hangtown. They were in business only one year after which Mr. Tallman became a freight hauler for the California Ice Co. in Sacramento. John Fountain remained in the soda water business for several more years, but moved his factory across the street from the 525 address, which he then used as his home.

Front: D.L. FONSECA & CO.
Re: JAMAICA / CHAMPAGNE BEER / S.F.

*Round, Smooth Base
Applied Top
Cobalt, $3600.00 - 2017
Green
Aqua
Rare in any Color
Circa: 1871
Locale: San Francisco
Note: Generally found in the S.F. Bay area, I know of 1 aqua example coming from Marin Co.*

History: David L. Fonseca was mainly listed as a physician, his history shows he must have been a quack, staying one step ahead of the law. In the 18 years (1874-1890) that he was listed as being in business, he moved his place of business 9 times, and his residence the same. That included moving from S.F. to Oakland and back again twice. In 1879 he was listed as a collector for the Odorless Excavation Apparatus Co., which cleaned out cisterns and out houses. In 1885-1886 he was listed as the manufacturer of Triumph Bitters, doing business at 17 Ellis St. S.F. In 1887 he again is listed as a Physician, but changed his name to D.L. De Fonseca, not to use his old name again. Judging from this guys history, the rare bottle bearing his name could have held about anything, including soda water. The ad to the right ran for only about one month in 1871. He sold his product out of Schord's Saloon, 531 California St. S.F. So the bottle above should date from 1871 only.

Front: G. G. (block letters) / MERCED

*Round, Smooth Base
Applied Top
Aqua, $375.00 - 2010
Rare
Circa: 1874-1881
Locale: Merced, Cal.*

HISTORY: Giovanni Galliano was the proprietor of the Merced Soda Works, Which was located on the corner of 18th and J Sts. from 1874-1881. In 1882 Galliano decided to move to Fresno, where with partner Frank Borello operated the Fresno Soda Works until 1893. He then moved back to Merced and became a grocer.

Front: GEYSER / SODA
Re: NATURAL / MINERAL / WATER / FROM / LITTON
       SPRINGS / SONOMA CO CAL

Round, Smooth Base
Applied and Tooled Top
Aqua
Scarce
Circa: 1886 - 1893
Locale: San Francisco

HISTORY: Litton Springs was located 4 miles north of
    Healdsburg in Sonoma Co. Cal. Listings as follows,
    1886 Litton Springs Company, B.M. Hungerford manager,
         Office 152 New Montgomery
    1887 Litton Springs Mineral Water Co., William B. Moore,
         manager, 152 New Montgomery
    1888 Litton Springs Mineral Water, Geo. E. Madison
         manager, 152 New Montgomery
    1889-93 Litton Springs Mineral Water Co. Louis Lowe, Jr.
         manager, 152 New Montgomery
    1894 See Lytton Geyser Soda Springs

Front: GEYSER / SODA / SPRINGS
Re: NATURAL / MINERAL WATER

Round, Smooth Base
Applied and Tooled Top
Lime Green
Aqua
Common in Aqua
Ex. Rare in Green
Circa: 1891-1898
Locale: San Francisco

HISTORY: The Geyser Soda Springs was first discovered by a hunter in
    1847. It is located about 4 miles from Geyserville in Sonoma Co. Cal.
    1891-92 Geyser Soda Company, E.L. Lowe Proprietor, 152 Montgomery
    1893-94 Geyser Soda Company, 29 Stuart
    1895-96 Geyser Water Company, R.H. Curry manager, Mineral Water, 41 Stevenson
    1896-97 Geyser Water Company, R.M. Horton manager, Mineral Water, 43 Stevenson
    No further listings

Front: GEYSER / NATURAL BOILED / MINERAL WATER (in round plate)

Round, Smooth Base
Tooled Top
Aqua
Rare
Circa: 1897-1898
Locale: San Francisco

HISTORY: See Geyser Soda Springs
    We assume the Natural Boiled is derived from the temperature of
    water as it came out of the spring. It ranged from 55 degrees
    Fahrenheit to 212 degrees.

Front: J. N. GERDES / S.F.
Re: MINERAL / WATER

8 Sided, Smooth Base
Applied Top
Aqua, $100.00 - 2019
Lime Green, $450.00 - 2007
Lt. Green, $350.00 - 2021
Common in Aqua
Rare in Shades of Green
Circa: 1873-1877
Locale: San Francisco
Note: This bottle is found all over the S.F. Bay area with examples coming from Suisun City and Benicia.

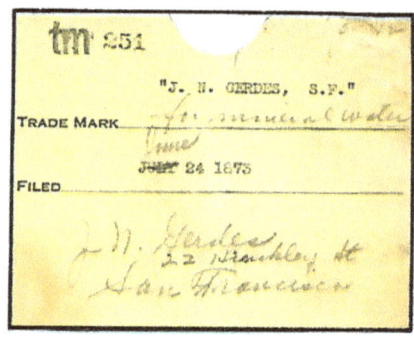

HISTORY: John N. Gerdes first appeared in the soda water business in the 1860's as a driver for the California Soda Works.
  1873-1875 Gerdes, John N., proprietor San Francisco Soda Works, 22 Hinckley
  1876-1877 Gerdes, John N., proprietor San Francisco Soda Works, 733 Union
             Gerdes, Henry, soda manufacturer with John N. Gerdes
In 1877 the company was taken over by Henry Gerdes and William Bruning, until 1880, at which time Bruning bought out Gerdes. There is no further mention of John Gerdes in the soda water business after 1877. In 1873, John N. Gerdes trade marked his name for mineral water. See above.

Front: GHIRARDELLI'S / BRANCH / OAKLAND

Round, Smooth Base
Applied Top
Green
Cobalt, $1000.00 - 2017
* $600.00 - 2021*
Ex. Rare in Green
Scarce in Cobalt
Circa: 1863-1869
Locale: Oakland, Cal.
Note: Ad at right circa 1869, below 1854.

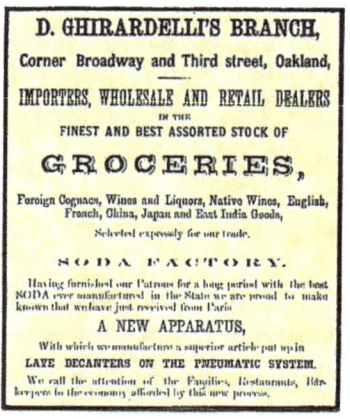

HISTORY: Domenico Ghirardelli got his start as a grocer in S.F. in 1850, located on Battery between Broadway and Vallejo. Ghirardelli & Co. was established in 1852, at which time Ghirardelli & Cox were listed in the confection business at 194 Washington St. In 1854 Mrs. Ghirardelli became the proprietor of the business and expanded to include syrups, liquors, coffee and soda water. Some time in 1853 Mr. Ghirardelli started a branch in Oakland at the corner of Third and Broadway. From 1863 thru 1869 he was listed as being importers, wholesale and retail dealers in groceries, foreign wines and liquors, English, French, China, Japan and East India goods, all while maintaining a soda factory. In 1870 he moved his business to the corner of Broadway and 7TH, and due to increasing business, devoted this store to the hardware and crockery business.

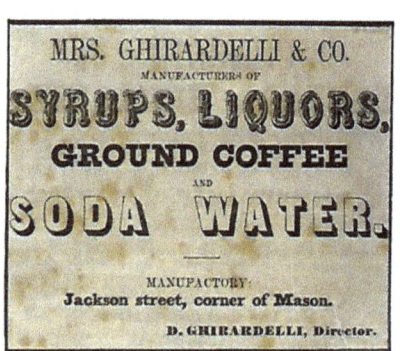

Front: GOLDEN GATE (in rect. plate)

Round, Iron Pontil and Smooth Base
Applied Top
Cobalt: I.P., $1000.00 - 2009
Teal Green, I.P., $325.00 - 2017
Teal Green, S.B., $280.00 - 2010
Green, S.B., $550.00 - 2021
Green, I.P., $425.00 - 2021
Yellow Olive
Ex. Rare in Blue and Yellow Olive
Scarce in other Colors
Varient: Non slug
Circa: 1850's to 1860s
Locale: Yankee Jim's and San Francisco

HISTORY: The majority of the pontiled examples of this bottle have been dug in Yankee Jim's and Forest Hill in Placer County, Cal. The smooth base, non slug plate varients are mostly found in the San Francisco Bay area with examples coming from Vallejo, Oakland, Napa and Suisun City. Some of what follows is conjecture, but it is based on extensive field excavations and newspaper research.

James Cartwright was one of the first pioneers to come to Yankee Jim's. He arrived in 1850 and set up a miners supply store. By 1852 he was established as the proprietor of a billiard and bowling parlor known as the Golden Gate Saloon. His business thrived until June of 1852, when the business portion of Yankee Jim's was destroyed by fire. Within six weeks the town was being rebuilt and a new brick building was being erected to house the Golden Gate Saloon.

Yankee Jim's was fast becoming one of the most prominent towns in Placer County. In July of 1853 a Col. McClure called a meeting of all the local miners for the purpose of establishing laws and water rights for miners. The meeting was the largest assembly ever held in the area and took place at Cartright & Pellygroves Golden Gate Saloon.

In early 1854 a second story was added to the Saloon building. The year 1857 stands out as the most important one politically in the history of Yankee Jim's. In June the state Democratic Convention was held there. The town population doubled to 2000 while the convention was in session. All the important events where held at the Golden Gate Saloon. Yankee Jim's went into decline in the late 1850's, and another fire in 1862 sealed its fate. It never recovered and faded away like many other early Gold Rush mining camps.

That's enough for the history lesson, lets get to the bottle digging. By the mid 1990's Max Bell and his partners had secured permission for about 90% of the property where the town site once stood. As the excavations progressed they got a clear picture of where the hotels, saloons and other prominent buildings once stood. 100's of bottles were found, but what stood out was the large number of Golden Gate sodas that where unearthed. They came from most of the business buildings and at least 10 mint specimens were found behind the Golden Gate Saloon site. These were all iron pontiled. There was an early soda bottling works in Yankee Jim's and behind this over 50 broken Golden Gate sodas were found. This is very unusual to find such a heavy concentration of one brand in one location unless they were bottled and used there. The only other dig that comes to mind where so many of the same bottle were found was a hole in the Benicia Arsenal where over 50 McGee bottles from Benicia were found.

Now for more speculation. James Folger and his two brothers arrived in California in 1849. By May of 1850 they were in San Francisco, and being that James was only 14 years old, Henry and Edward decided to leave him in San Francisco while they went to mine gold. James already had been trained as a carpenter and William Bovee hired him to build the first wind powered mill in San Francisco. It was known as the Pioneer Spice Mills. In 1851 after the mill was completed he headed for the mines to join his brothers. They were mining in the Yankee Jim's area of Placer County. He took with him samples of coffee and spices from Bovee and upon arriving in Yankee Jim's he opened the Empire Store selling all forms of miners supplies. His ads are often seen in the Placer Herald newspaper starting in 1852. The store was located near the Golden Gate Saloon.

James made a large gold strike and by 1859 he was back in San Francisco and became partners with William Bovee in the Pioneer Spice Mill. In 1859 Bovee sold his interest in the mill to Ira Marden. Folger and Marden ran the mill until Folger bought out Marden and renamed it J.A. Folger Co. This date would be between 1866 and 1872, info was conflicting on this. One thing that is easily noticed about Folgers brands is that they all state "FOLGER'S GOLDEN GATE" on them. This is pure speculation but James Folger spent his early years in Yankee Jim's and he may have been the one who started the Golden Gate soda brand that was no doubt sold out of the Golden Gate Saloon in Yankee Jim's. When he left for San Francisco in 1859 he must have taken the brand with him.

About this same time, early 1860's, the smooth base Golden Gate soda appears. The newer bottle had a much larger distribution area, as only the pontiled bottle was found in Yankee Jim's and Forest Hill. The newer Golden Gate bottle is found in different spots all around the bay area. This all might be just wishful thinking but it is food for thought.

Front: GOLDEN WEST / NAPA / COUNTY / NAT'L SPRINGS
Re: NATURAL / MINERAL WATER / NAPA / COUNTY, CAL.

Round, Smooth Base
Tooled Top
Aqua
Rare
Circa: 1895-1897
Locale: San Francisco

History: The years of 1895 thru 1897 were the only years this company was listed as being in business. See Herve and Somps, See Golden West Napa County Soda Springs.

Front: GOLDEN WEST / NAPA / COUNTY / SODA SPRINGS
Re: GOLDEN WEST / NAPA / COUNTY / SODA SPRINGS

Round, Smooth Base
Tooled Top
Aqua
Ex. Rare
Circa: 1895-1897
Locale: San Francisco

HISTORY: See previous bottle.

Please see addendum by Mike Southworth

Front: GREENWOOD / AND / MORLEY / VICTORIA / B.C.

Round, Smooth Base
Applied Top
Aqua
Rare
Circa: 1871-1879
Locale: Victoria, B.C.

HISTORY: from 1871 thru 1879 Greenwood and Morley were listed as manufacturers of soda water, lemonade, ginger beer, bitters and all kinds of syrups. Their place of business was listed as being on Lower Yates St., in Victoria, B.C.

Front: GREENWOOD / AND / MORLEY / VICTORIA / B.C.
         (embossed vertically)

Round, Smooth Base
Applied Top
Aqua
Rare
Circa: 1871-1879
Locale: Victoria, B.C.

HISTORY: See above bottle.

Front: H.D. / ALBANY, O.

Round, Smooth Base
Applied Top
Aqua
Ex. Rare
Circa: 1875-1879
Locale: Albany, Oregon

HISTORY: The "H.D." stood for Hoffman, Davis, which were located on the north side of First St. in Albany, Ore. It is thought that the H.D. was bottled at the Albany Soda Works which later became the City Bottling Co.

Unlisted Golden West Soda variation courtesy Mike Southworth

Unlisted soda. Variant of the Golden West at the top of page 37 in the current Markota book updated by Higgins Jan. 20, 2020. book. Now listed as a variant where the reverse is NATURAL/MINERAL WATER/NAPA/COUNTY CAL. It is also extremely Rare with the same dates of 1895-1897.

Variances of Golden West Soda

Shown on page 36: GOLDEN WEST/NAPA/county/ NAT'L SPRINGS
NATURAL/MINERAL WATER/ NAPA/ COUNTY, CAL.

Top page age 37: GOLDEN WEST/NAPA/ county/ SODA SPRINGS
GOLDEN WEST/NAPA/ county/ SODA SPRINGS

Mike Southworth bottle: GOLDEN WEST/NAPA/ county/ SODA SPRINGS
NATURAL/MINERAL WATER/NAPA/ COUNTY, CAL.

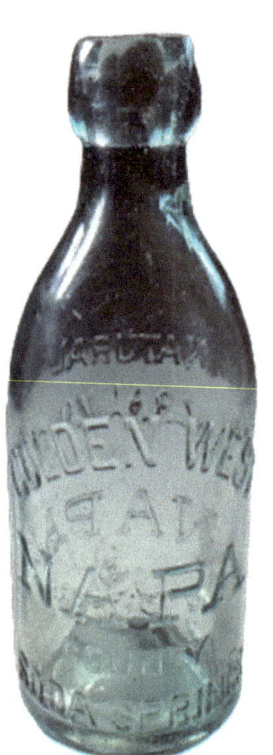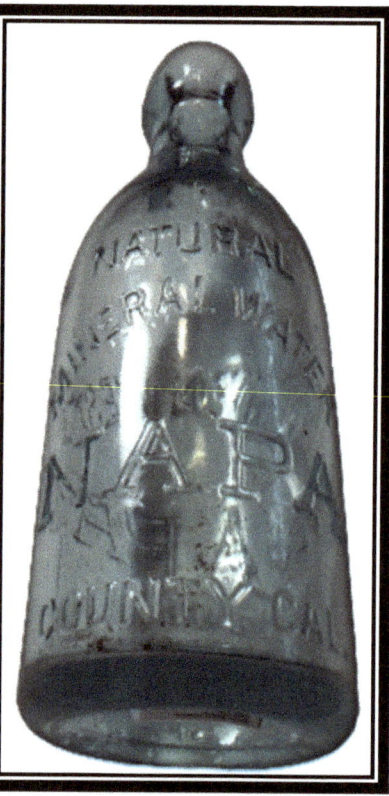

Above images of Mike Southworth's Golden West bottle

Addendum 37-A

Front: G M HENDERSON / BONANZA / MINERAL WATER / MENDOCINO / CAL.

Round, Smooth Base
Applied and Tooled Top
Aqua, $475.00 - 2021
Rare
Circa: 1890-1892
Locale: Mendocino, Cal.

HISTORY: The Bonanza Springs was located about 2 miles from Seigler's Springs, 6 miles from Glenbrook and 8 miles from Lower Lake. The water from this spring was bottled for only 2 years.

Front: H & H / HONOLULU

Round, Smooth Base
Applied Top
Aqua
Green
Rare
Circa: 1860's
Locale: Honolulu, Hawaii

HISTORY: In 1863 H.R. Hollister and Hyland had established their soda water business. In 1868 Hollister had started the Hollister Soda Works, and in 1894 it was incorporated into the Consolidated Soda Works Ltd. By 1873, Hollister & Co. had become a wholesale druggist and tobacconist, but still retained their "Aerated Water Works" at 73 Hotel St. in Honolulu.

Front: E. HERVE & P. SOMPS / PROPS / 622 LAGUNA ST. / S.F. CAL.
Re: NATURAL / MINERAL WATER / FROM THE / GOLDEN WEST SPRINGS / NAPA / COUNTY CAL.

Round, Smooth Base
Tooled Top
Aqua, $130.00 - 2021
Rare
Varient: Hutch
Circa: 1895-1897
Locale: San Francisco, Cal.

HISTORY: See Walter's Napa County Soda
1895-96 Herve and Somps, Mineral Water, 622 Laguna
1896-97 Golden West Springs Co. Eugene Herve and Pierre Somps, proprietors, 622 Laguna
1897   No further listing of Herve and Somps together. Also there is no further listing of the Golden West Springs Co.

In 1895 Herve and Somps started the Golden West Springs Co. in San Francisco and apparently obtained the mold for their bottles from J.Somps and J. Meillette, who used this same bottle from 1892 to 1895 and added their name to it. This same bottle was used by F. Paillet from 1901 to 1906. We also believe that Herve and Somps were getting their supply of mineral water from the Walters Soda Springs in Napa County and bottling it under the name of Natural Mineral Water from the Golden West Springs, Napa County, Cal. The reason being is that the Golden West Springs never did exist in Napa County.

Front: E. HIGGINS / OROVILLE

Round, Smooth Base
Applied Top
Aqua, $250.00 - 2021
Rare
Varient: Hutch
Circa: 1875-1887
Locale: Oroville, Cal.
Note: Examples are known from the Northern California towns of Chico, Red Bluff, Oroville and Marysville, and from the mining town of Grass Valley in Nevada Co.

HISTORY: Edward Higgins was the proprietor of the Oroville Soda Works, which was located on Montgomery St. in the years 1875-1887. These dates may vary a few years due to lack of info.

Front: HOFFMAN & JOSEPH / "LION" / ALBANY, OGN.

Round, Smooth Base
Tooled Top
Aqua, $170.00 - 2021
Rare
Circa: 1880-1887
Locale: Albany, Oregon

HISTORY: in the 1880's, John Hoffman and Julius Joseph were listed as a Soda Works, cigars, tobacco, groceries and candy manufacturers in Albany, Oregon. In 1882 they applied for a trade mark on this bottle. Ad above is circa 1881.

Front: HOGAN & THOMPSON / SAN FRANCISCO (in slug plate)
Re: UNION GLASS WORKS / PHILA.

Round, Iron Pontil
Applied Top
Cobalt, $5000.00 - 2021
Ex. Rare
Circa: 1854 (approx)
Locale: San Francisco
Note: One of these rare bottles was dug at Yankee Jim's in Placer County in the mid 1990's.

HISTORY: 1854 Hogan, P.J., Union Soda Factory, Union Place
Hogan, H., Union Soda Factory, Union Place
Thompson, Geo., Union Soda Factory, Union Place
There were no city directories published for San Francisco in 1853 or 1855, so the years Hogan & Thompson were actually in business could overlap the 1854 date either way by a year. The 1856 directory states that Geo. Thompson was in business with J. McEwin manufacturing soda water on the north side of Union St. near Stockton. No further mention of Hogan.

Front: HAWAIIAN / SODA / WORKS / HONOLULU

    Round, Smooth Base
    Tooled Top
    Aqua
    Rare
    Circa: 1890-1900's
    Locale: Honolulu, Hawaii

HISTORY: No info at this time.

Front: HOLLISTER / & CO. / HONOLULU

    Round, Smooth Base
    Applied Top
    Aqua, $600.00 - 2021
    Scarce in Aqua
    Ex. Rare in Blue
    Variemt: Codd, Round Bottom Hutch
    Circa: 1870's
    Locale: Honolulu, Hawaii

HISTORY: See H & H Honolulu

Front: HOLLISTER / SODA / WORKS / A. MANS

    Round, Smooth Base
    Applied Top
    Aqua, $500.00 - 2017, $210.00 - 2021
    Rare
    Circa: 1870's
    Locale: Hollister, Cal.

HISTORY: Info on Alfred Mans is scarce. He was the proprietor of the French Hotel and Restaurant in the 1870's, in Hollister. In the 1880's he was listed as the proprietor of the French Saloon and Restaurant. Also in the late 1870's he was in the liquor business on 5th St. in Hollister. It was probably at this time he was selling soda water as a side business.

Front: I. HOUGLAND / LEADVILLE / COL.
Base: I.H.

    Round, Smooth Base
    Applied Top
    Aqua
    Rare
    Variant: Hutch
    Circa: 1879-1884
    Locale: Leadville, Colorado

HISTORY: Isacc Hougland was manufacturing and bottling soda water in Leadville from 1879 to 1884. He was located at 132 West Third St. South above Pine.

Front: I. HOUGLAND
Base: H.

    Round, Smooth Base
    Applied Top
    Aqua
    Rare
    Circa: 1879-1884
    Locale: Leadville, Colo.

HISTORY: See previous bottle

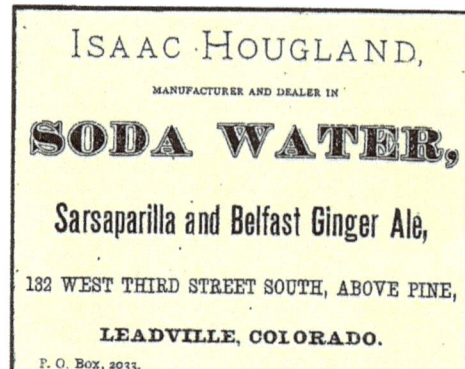

Front: HUMBOLDT / ARTESIAN / MINERAL WATER
Re: EUREKA, CAL. (embossed vertically)

    Round, Smooth Base
    Aqua, Tooled Top, 220.00 - 2021
    Applied and Tooled Top
    Scarce
    Varient: Hutch
    Circa: 1893-1897
    Locale: San Francisco, Cal.

History: 1893-1897, Humboldt Mineral Water Co., J.P. Monroe Manager, Stephen Jackson Agent, Third St. S.F. Label below was trade marked in 1892 by J.P. Monroe of Eureka. Ad below right is also circa 1892

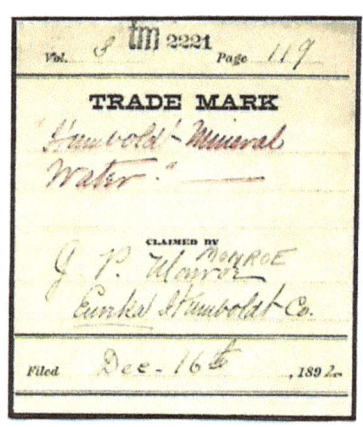

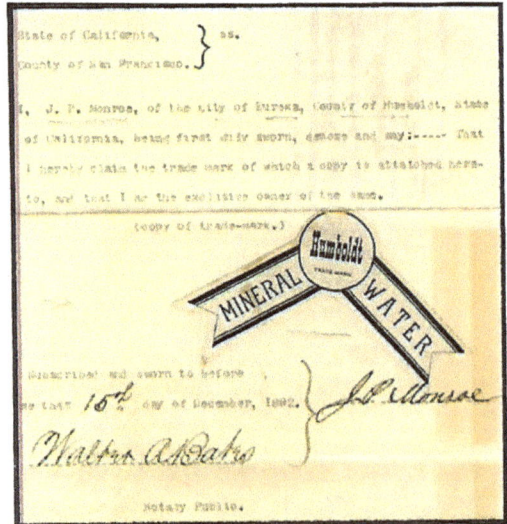
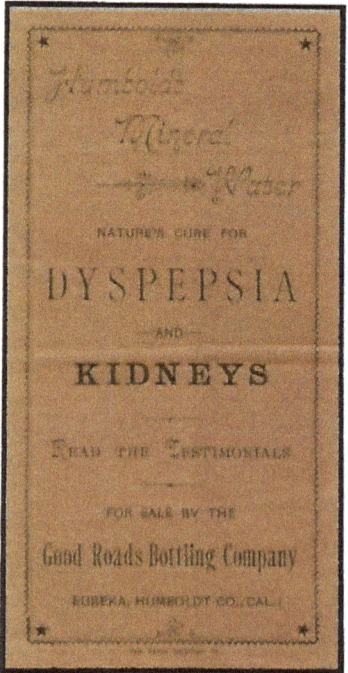

Front: ITALIAN / SODA WATER / MANUFACTORY / SAN FRANCISCO
Re: UNION GLASS WORKS / PHILA.

Round, Iron Pontil
Applied Top
Cobalt, $800.00 - 2010
Teal Blue, $5500.00 - 2017
Blue green, $650.00 - 2017
Green, $1300.00 - 2010
 Varient: Reverse is Blank
  Deep Cobalt, $800.00 - 2018 (chip)
 Varient: Union Glass is slugged out
           COBALT, $1400.00 - 2021
 Varient: "WORKS" is spelled "WOKS"
Scarce
Circa: 1856 - 1863
Locale: San Francisco
Note: A green one was dug in Yankee
 Jim's and a blue example came out
 Georgetown in the 1990's.

HISTORY: 1856-57 Italian Soda Factory, Joseph Spinoni proprietor cor. Powell and Filbert
            Established by Ghirardin in 1852 and reestablished by Spinoni in 1854
         1858-59 Spinoni, Joseph, Soda Factory, Stevenson near Annie
         1859-60 Spinoni, Joseph, Italian Soda Factory, Stevenson between 2nd and 3rd
         1860-61 Grellier, S. & Co., (J. McEwen) Italian Soda Works, 192 Stevenson
         1862-62 Grellier & Co. (Italian), 192 Stevenson
         In 1865 192 Stevenson was listed as the address of the California Soda Works,
            James McEwin, proprietor.

Front: J.B. / CENTRAL CITY / COL.
Base: L.G.Co.

Round, Smooth Base
Applied Top
Aqua
Ex. Rare
Circa: 1872-1892
Locale: Central City, Colo.

HISTORY: Joseph S. Beaman, was a bottler of beer, wine and soda
 water. His place of business was known as the City Bottling Works,
 no address given. No other info at this time.

Front: J.T. / ELKO / NEV.

Round, Smooth Base
Applied Top
Aqua, $3600.00 - 2015
Ex. Rare
Circa: 1869-1891
Locale: Elko, Nevada
Note: Most of the known specimens of this bottle came from the Elko area. One came from
 a collection in California and it is not known where it was found.

HISTORY: James Talbot probably began his soda water business in 1869. After
 20 plus years in business he sold it to James Dewar, and moved to Idaho.
 These bottles are very rare, so he probably used them for a very short time,
 most likely in the late 1870's.

Front: JACKSON'S / NAPA / SODA / SPRINGS
Re: NATURAL / MINERAL WATER

Round, Smooth Base
Applied Top
Aqua
Green
Teal Blue, $1900.00 - 2019
Blue, $550.00 - 2019
Cobalt, $650.00 - 2019
Common in Aqua
Scarce in Shades of Blue
Rare in Shades of Green
Varient: "A" on Base
Circa: 1873-1875
Locale: San Francisco
Note: This is the earliest version of the Jackson line.
      There are many varients, of which most will follow.

HISTORY: see Wood's Napa Soda
    Col. John P. Jackson assumed ownership of the Napa Soda Springs in 1870 for
    $20,000.00. It was located on a hill side about 5 miles northeast of Napa City.
    Col. Jacksom operated the Resort and Springs until he passed away in 1901.
    The whole complex burned in 1944, and has never been rebuilt. In its heyday
    the bottling house was producing 200-300 dozen bottles of water a day, which
    were then shipped to San Francisco to be distributed all over the West and beyond.

    Bottle embossing was trade marked in 1872 by John Jackson, Napa City.
    The Label was trade marked in 1892 also by John Jackson. See below.

Front: JACKSON'S / NAPA / SODA / SPRINGS
Re: NATURAL / MINERAL WATER THIS BOTTLE / IS NEVER SOLD

   Round, Smooth Base
   Tooled Top
   Aqua
   Common
   Varient: "A" on base
   Circa: 1885-1895
   Locale: San Francisco

HISTORY: *See previous bottle*

Front: JACKSON'S / NAPA / SODA
Re: A NATURAL / MINERAL WATER / JACKSON'S / THIS BOTTLE / IS NEVER SOLD
Basr: P.C.G.W.

   Round, Smooth Base
   Tooled and Applied Top
   Lime Green
   Aqua
   Common in Aqua
   Rare in Colors
   Varient: minus This Bottle is Never Sold
       "This" is misspelled TIHS
       Crown Top
   Circa: 1895-1906
   Locale: San Francisco

HISTORY: *Agents for Jackson's Napa Soda in S.F.*
   1873-1874, Andrew Jackson, 18 ½ Geary
   1875-1876, John P. Jackson, 130 Geary
   1876-1877, Edward P. Jeffries, 130 Geary
   1878-1882, John T. Ward, 130 Geary
   1882-1883, Cutler & Pearson, 11 Drum
   1884-1888, William A. Brown, 159 New Montgomery
   1888-1889, Charles H. Jackson, 159 New Montgomery
   1889-1892, John P. Jackson, 159 New Montgomery
   1892-1893, George H.T. Jackson, 159 New Montgomery
   1893-1898, George H.T. Jackson, 619 Howard
   1898-1904, George H.T. Jackson, 147-149 New Montgomery
   1904-1905, George H.T. Jackson, 644 Howard
   1906-   George H.T. Jackson, 760 Golden Gate Ave.

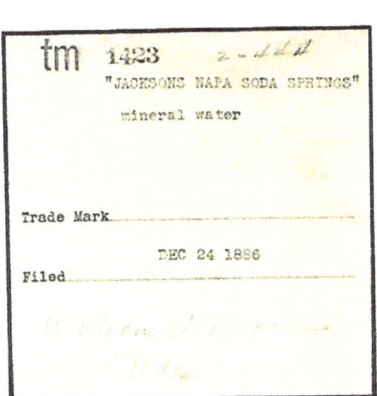

Front: JACKSON'S / NAPA / SODA / SPRINGS
Re: NATURAL / MINERAL WATER
Base: B & Co

   Round, Smooth Base
   Applied and Tooled Top
   Base: See at Right
   Aqua
   Lime Green
   Rare
   Circa: 1886-1887
   Locale: San Francisco

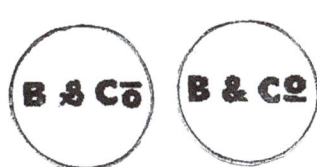

HISTORY: *From 1884 to 1887 William A. Brown was the agent for the Napa Soda Depot at 159 New Montgomery. Mr. Brown applied for a trade mark for this bottle 1886. It was used for about one year only.*

Front: JACKSON'S / NAPA / SODA / SPRINGS
Re: NATURAL / MINERAL WATER / B.F. CONNOLLY

Round, Smooth Base
Applied Top
Aqua
Lime Green
Rare
Circa: 1873-1884
Locale: Petaluma, Cal.

HISTORY: B.F. Connolly was the agent for Jackson's Napa Soda in Petaluma. See Connolly & Bro. S.F. for more info.

Front: JACKSON'S / NAPA / SODA / SPRINGS
Re: NATURAL / MINERAL WATER
Base: C & P

Round, Smooth base
Applied and Tooled Top
Aqua
Rare
Circa: 1882-1883
Locale: San Francisco

HISTORY: Cutler & Pearson were the agents for Jackson's Napa Soda in San Francisco from 1882-1883, located at 11 Drum.

Front: JACKSON'S / NAPA / SODA / SPRINGS
Re: NATURAL / MINERAL WATER / M. SILVA

Round, Smooth base
Applied and Tooled Top
Aqua, $70.00 - 2021
Lime Green
Scarce
Circa: 1878-1890
Locale: Napa, Cal.
Note: These are generally found in the Napa Valley area with a few turning up a little further away. Petaluma, Vallejo, Benicia and Oakland have yeilded examples.

HISTORY: Manuel Silva was the proprietor of the Napa Soda Works and the agent for Jackson's Napa Soda in Napa County. His business was located at the corner of Main and Stuart St. The Napa Soda Works was first started in 1878 and he bottled as many as 600 dozen bottles a month.

Front: JACKSON'S / NAPA / SODA / SPRINGS
Re: NATURAL / MINERAL WATER / ED. HENRY

Round, Smooth Base
Applied and Tooled Top
Aqua, Applied Top, $375.00 - 2017
Rare
Varient: Crown top, and Hutch
Circa: 1890-1918
Locale: Napa, Cal.
Note: Found in the same areas as the previous bottle.

HISTORY: Ed Henry took over as agent for Jackson's Napa Soda from M. Silva. He was in business until around 1918.

Front: JACKSON'S / NAPA / SODA / SPRINGS
Re: NATURAL / MINERAL WATER / F.M. / VALLEJO

Round, Smooth Base
Applied Top
Aqua, $700.00 - 2017
Ex. Rare
Circa: 1873-1885 (approx)
Locale: Vallejo, Cal.
Note: These very rare bottles generally are only found in Vallejo and neighboring towns Napa and Benicia.

HISTORY: Fred Michaelis was the Vallejo agent for Jackson's Napa Soda.

Front: JACKSON'S / NAPA / SODA / SPRINGS
Re: NATURAL / MINERAL WATERS / S.P. & CO.

Round, Smooth Base
Applied Top
Aqua
Ex. Rare
Circa: 1873-1885 (approx.)
Locale: Pasadena, Cal.

HISTORY: This bottle was used by M.A. Sattley and A.J. Page in Pasadena. They were the general agents for Jackson's Napa Soda in Southern Cal.

Front: JACKSON'S / NAPA / SODA / SPRINGS
Re: NATURAL / MINERAL WATER / A. BRESSON

Round, Smooth Base
Applied Top
Aqua
Ex. Rare
Circa: 1880's
Locale: Fairfax and San Rafael, Cal.
Note: Known specimens of this bottle have all been found in Marin County.

HISTORY: A. Bresson was the agent for Jackson's Soda in Marin County in the 1880's.

Front: JERGENS & PRICE / BOTTLERS / HELENA, MONT. (in round plate)

Round, Smooth Base
Tooled Top
Aqua, $80.00 - 2021
Scarce
Varient: Hutch
Circa: late 1880's (approx.)
Locale: Helena, Montana

HISTORY: Jurgens and Price were in business in Helena until around 1900.

Front: KELLY & HANRAHAN

> Round, Smooth Base
> Applied Top
> Aqua
> Ex. Rare
> Varient: "LEADVILLE, COL.", embossed under name
> Circa: 1878
> Locale: Leadville, Colorado

HISTORY: Kelly and Hanrahan were in business for only about one year. They were located on Main St. in Leadville.

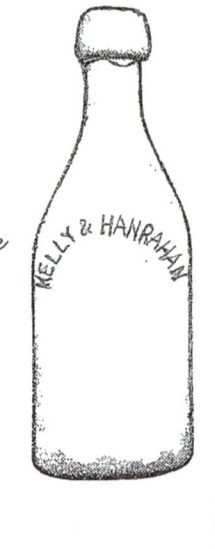

Front: KIMBALL & CO. (block letters)

> Round, Iron Pontil
> Applied Top
> Cobalt, $700.00 - 2017
> Scarce
> Circa: 1853=1856
> Locale: Marysville, Cal.
> Note: Generally found in the Marysville area, a few have been dug in the Northern Mines in the California Gold Country, including the small town of Dobbins.

HISTORY: Charles H. Kimball was listed in the soda water business from 1853 to 1856. From 1853 to 1855 his business was located on the corner of B and Front Sts., and in 1855 he was listed on B St., between Front and First St. In Sept. of 1856 he put his business up for sale, by then he was located on the corner of First and B St.

Front: E & JL

> Round, Smooth Base
> Applied Top
> Aqua, $1300.00 - 2021
> Ex. Rare
> Circa: 1867-1874
> Locale: Knights Ferry, Cal.
> Note: One example was dug in Modesto many years ago.

HISTORY: E. & J. Lodtmann are listed as being in the general merchandise and soda water manufacturing business in Knights Ferry from 1867 to 1874 or 1875. In the 1880's they took their expertise of the soda water trade to Santa Cruz, Cal. They bottled soda water there until the late 1880's and then ventured into the real estate business.

Front: B.R. LIPPINCOTT / STOCKTON (in slug plate)
Re: SUPERIOR MINERAL WATER / UNION GLASS WORKS

> 10 Sided Mug Base, Iron Pontil and Open Pontil
> Applied Top
> Cobalt, $1600.00 - 2013, $2200.00 - 2019
> Rare with Iron Pontil
> Ex. Rare with Open Pontil
> Circa: 1852-1858 (approx)
> Locale: Stockton, Cal.
> Note: I have not heard of any of these being found anywhere but in Stockton.

HISTORY: In the 1852 Stockton City Directory it lists Lippincott and Vaughn as syrup manufacturers, so maybe they did not start in the soda water business until 1853, but in the "History of San Joaquin County" it states that Lippincott and Vaughn started the soda water business in July, 1852.

Front: L &V (block letters)

> Round, Iron Pontil
> Applied Top
> Green, $400.00 - 2009
> Scarce
> Circa: 1852-1857
> Locale: Stockton, Cal.
> Note: Found in Stockton and Sacramento areas as well as Marysville.

HISTORY: See B.R. Lippincott
- 1852 Lippincott, B.R., firm of Lippincott and Vaughn, syrup Manufactory, corner Weber and San Joaquin
  Vaughn, A.F., firm of Lippincott and Vaughn, syrup Manufactory, corner Weber and San Joaquin
- 1856 Lippincott and Vaughn, Soda Factory, Weber opposite Plaza

In 1857 Charles Belding bought an interest in the business of his old employers, after he and John B. Vaughn, younger brother of A.F. Vaughn, made an unsuccessful attempt at manufacturing soda water at Murphy's, Cal. The company then became known as Lippincott and Belding.

Front: L & B (block letters)

> Round, Smooth Base
> Applied Top
> Aqua
> Green, $475.00 - 2017
> Varient: "B" is slugged over the "V"
>   Comes in the slope shoulder Pony shape
> Circa: 1857-1870
> Locale: Stockton and Marysville, Cal.

HISTORY: See B.R. Lippincott and L and V
- 1857-1870 Lippincott & Belding, Soda Water Manufacturers, cor Weber and San Joaquin in Stockton
- 1863-1870 Lippincott & Belding, Soda Water Manufacturers, cor 2nd St. & Virgin Alley, Marysville

---

Front: LOS ANGELES / SODA / & / MINERAL / WATER / FACTORY
Re: H.W. STOLL

> Round, Smooth Base
> Applied Top
> Aqua, $700.00 - 2019,
> $2200.00 - 2017
> Rare
> Circa: 1875-1884
> Locale: Los Angeles, Cal.
> Note: Usually found only in Southern Cal., both varients were dug in Anaheim in the 1970's.

HISTORY: Henry W. Stoll was in the soda water business from 1873 thru 1900. In 1873-1874 he was listed with W.H. Huber as being the proprietors of the Los Angeles Soda Works, at 13 Aliso St. From 1875-1884 he is listed as the sole proprietor at the same address. In 1878 he moved to 38 Sainsevain St. In 1884 he took on P.C. Stoll, his brother, as a partner and moved to 107 Sansevain St. H.W. Stoll & Co. remained there until 1900. In the late 1880's they were also listed as the proprietors of the Pasadena Soda Works at 219 S. Fair Oaks Ave.

Front: LYNDE & PUTNAM / MINERAL WATER / SAN FRANCISCO / CAL.A (in slug plate)
Re: UNION GLASS WORKS / PHILAD.A

Round, Open and Iron Pontil
Applied Top
Teal Green, I.P., $1000.00 - 2021
Cobalt, $1700.00 - 2021
Benicia Effect, $2200.00 - 2019
Scarce with Iron Pontil
Ex. Rare with Open Pontil
Varient: without Slug Plate
Circa: 1850-1851
Locale: San Francisco
Note: Found in the S.F. redevelopment areas, the mud flats around Benicia, and in early mining camps in the Gold Country.

HISTORY: Passengers J.D. Lynde and H.W. Putnam first arrived in San Francisco on a ship from Panama on March 27, 1850. They must have gone into the soda water business almost immediately.

1850 Lynde & Putnam, water dealers, Washington Place between Washington and Jackson Sts.

1851 Lynde & Putnam, Sansome St., between Jackson and Washington Sts.

October 2nd, 1851, first advertisement placed in a San Francisco newspaper cautioning "The public, and particularly mineral water dealers, are hereby cautioned against purchasing from anybody, mineral water bottles having the name of "LYNDE & PUTNAM" pressed on the side of the bottle. All such bottles belong to the subscribers, who have never disposed of any, and who require all for their trade. This notice is given because the subscribers have discovered that other persons are using said bottles for their own trade. LYNDE & PUTNAM".

February 18th, 1852, F.C. Chase & Co. places advertisement in newspaper as successors to Lynde & Putnam. Lynde & Putnam would be the first mineral water business in San Francisco to use embossed bottles. It makes one wonder if they had this planned out in advance and brought their bottles with them from the east.

Front: LYTTON / GEYSER / SODA / SPRINGS
Re: NATURAL / MINERAL WATER

Round, Smooth Base
Applied and Tooled Top
Aqua
Common
Circa: 1894-1899
Locale: San Francisco

HISTORY: 1893 See GEYSER SODA
1894 Lytton Springs Mineral Water Co., Phillip Kyle manager, office 41 2nd St.
1895 Lytton Springs Water Co., Edward B. Strong general manager 41 2nd
1896 Lytton Springs Water Co., Lytton's Geyser Soda, Lytton's California Seltzer, Isaac Burke manager, office 41 2nd
1897-98 Lytton Springs Water Co., William H. Bone manager, Office 218 McCallister
1899 Lytton Springs Water Co., 33 2nd

Front: LITTON'S / MINERAL / WATER
Re: HEALDSBURG, CAL. (embossed vertically)

   Round, Smooth Base
   Applied Top
   Aqua, $1500.00 - 2010
   Ex. Rare
   Circa: 1870's
   Locale: Healdsburg, Cal.
   Note: This very rare bottle has been dug in Santa Rosa and Healdsburg, Cal. The bottle is a little bigger than your normal soda bottle. I would say it's about a pint in size.

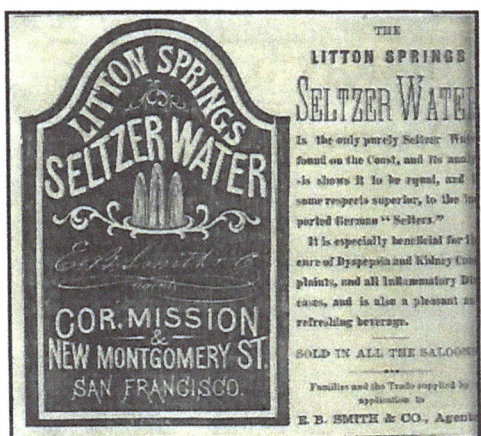

HISTORY: See previous bottle.
         Ad is circa 1876.

Front: M (in a Circle)

   Round, Smooth Base
   Applied Top
   Deep Aqua, $375.00 - 2017
   Ex. Rare
   Circa: Late 1870's to Early 1880's
   Locale: Stockton, Cal.
   Note: This bottle has been found in many Delta towns with water access. Suisun City, Benicia, Martinez, Concord, Antioch, Pacheco and Stockton have yielded examples.

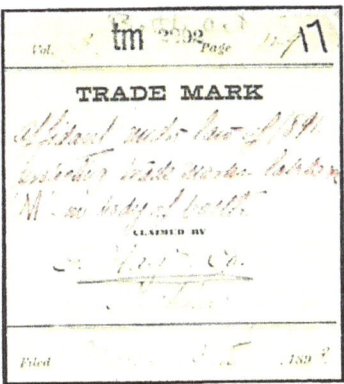

HISTORY: This embossing pattern was trade marked in 1893 by E. May & Co., Stockton, Cal. It was for bottles holding soda, cider and other similar items.

Front: M. MADSON / LARAMIE / W.T.
Base: A. & D.H.C.

   Round, Smooth Base
   Applied Top
   Aqua
   Ex. Rare
   Circa: Early 1880's
   Locale: Laramie, Wyoming

History: No info available for this bottle.

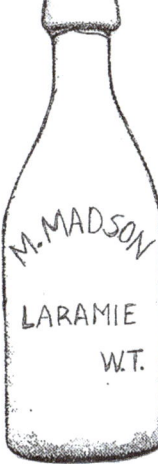

Front: MARTINELLI'S / SODA WORKS / M.S.

Round, Smooth Base
Applied Top
Aqua, $230.00 - 2017
Scarce
Circa: 1875-1890 (approx)
Locale: Watsonville, Cal.
Note: Stephen Martinelli trade marked this embossing pattern for his bottles in 1875. He also trade marked the "APPLE CIDER" label in 1885. Commonly found in the Watsonville area, one was dug in San Leandro in the mid 1980's.

HISTORY: The company was founded in 1868 selling hard cider. Martinelli then expanded into the soda and mineral water business in the 1870's. This bottle probably held both his cider and mineral water products.

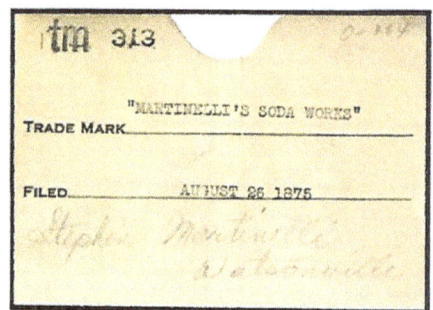

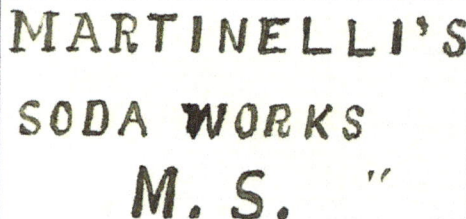

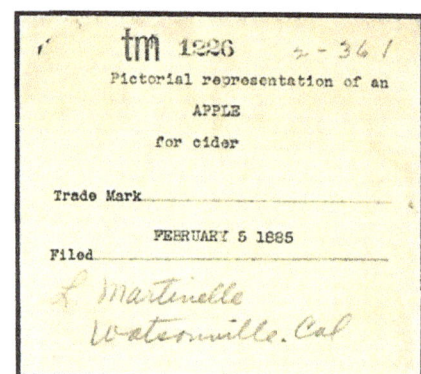

Front: M & D / SALT LAKE CITY / UTAH
Re: A. & D.H.C.

Round, Smooth Base
Applied Top
Aqua
Rare
Circa: Late 1870's to Early 1880's
Locale: Salt Lake City, Utah

HISTORY: M & D stands for W. Marsden and H. Denhalter. They had a soda factory on Commercial St. in Salt Lake City from around 1878 to 1881. This bottle is a territorial bottle as Utah became a state in 1896.

Front: H. MAU & CO. / EUREKA / NEVADA

Round, Smooth Base
Applied and Tooled Top
Aqua, $275.00 - 2009
Common
Varient: misspelled "MAW", Ex. Rare
    $2400.00 - 2007, $350.00 - 2021
Circa: 1882-1885
Locale: Eureka, Nevada
Note: Mau bottles are found primarily in the town of Eureka, with many of the 100+ known unearthed in nearby mining camps.

HISTORY: In the 1870's Henry Mau and F.M. Heitman were listed as being in the liquor and saloon business in Eureka. From 1882 to 1886 they were listed as being the proprietors of the San Francisco Brewery and Soda Works. After 1886 they were still listed as the proprietors of the San Francisco Brewery and saloon, but no mention of a soda works. Misspelled bottle circa 1882.

Front: MEAD

8 Sided, Smooth Base
Applied Top
Aqua, $140.00 - 2017
Rare
Circa: 1870's
Locale: San Francisco

HISTORY: No info available on this bottle. It may be a reworked J.N. Gerdes mold.

Front: MERRIAM'S

Round, Iron Pontil
Applied Top
Cobalt, $2800.00 - 2021
Ex. Rare
Circa: 1852-1856
Locale: Sonora, Cal.

HISTORY: J. Merriam and J.L. Merriam started their soda works in Sonora in 1852. It changed ownership many times over the years until Michael Terzich bought it and he operated it for many years. It was one of the longest continuous operating soda works in California.

Front: McEWIN
Re: SAN FRANCISCO

10 Sided, Smooth Base
Applied Top
Aqua, Clear, Amethyst
Aqua, $325.00 - 2021
Scarce
Circa: 1863-1870
Locale: San Francisco
Note: James McEwin trade marked this embossing pattern for his lemon soda bottles in 1867. This bottle is found in many different towns in bay area including Vallejo, Benicia and Suisun City.

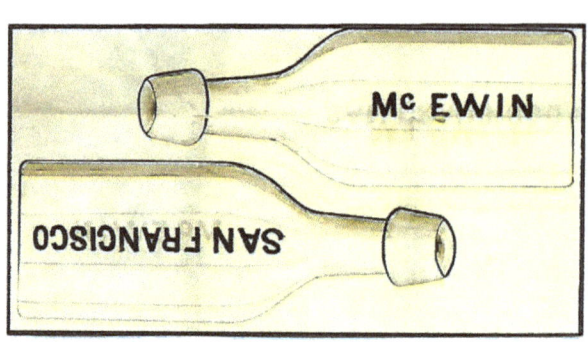

HISTORY: James McEwin started in the soda water business around 1856 in partnership with George C. Thompson as owner of the Union Mineral Water Works. In 1860 he was a partner with S. Grellier at the Italian Soda Works. In 1862 he was in the wagon transport business.
1863-1864, McEwin, James, Proprietor California Soda Works, 192 Stevenson
1865-1866, McEwin, James, California Soda Works, 192 Stevenson
1867-1869, McEwin, James, California Soda Works, 194 Stevenson
1869-1870, McEwin, James, California Soda Works, 190 Stevenson
Then in 1871 he became the proprietor of the Bay City Soda Water Co. See Bay City.
On June 1, 1867, The San Francisco Chronicle ran an ad from James McEwin warning people that deal and purchase used bottles about using bottles with his name on them. See ad below.

TO SODA MANUFACTURERS AND All Others Dealing In Bottles.

YOU ARE HEREBY CAUTIONED against filling, using, dealing with or trafficking in any bottles of the following make or description:
My bottles are of the ordinary sized Soda Bottle, each of which is pentagonal, or ten-sided, on one of which sides is blown in raised letters "McEWIN," and on the opposite, or reverse side, "SAN FRANCISCO."
All are hereby informed that on the 23d day of May last I filed in the office of the Secretary of State, of California, a description and drawings of the above described bottles, and the words thereon as aforesaid, claiming the same as my Trade Mark.
Any person hereafter found using, claiming, or dealing with any bottle of the above description, will be prosecuted to the full extent of the law.
JAMES McEWEN.
San Francisco, June 1st, 1867.   jy16-1m*

Front: MERRITT & CO. / HELENA / MONTANA
Base: M & Co.

Round, Smooth Base
Tooled Top
Aqua, $100.00 - 2007
Rare
Circa: Late 1880's to Early 1890's
Locale: Helena, Montana

HISTORY: No info on this bottle at this time.

Front: B.J. McGEE / BENICIA

Round, Smooth Base
Applied Top
Aqua, $275.00 - 2021
Lt. Green, $600.00 - 2010
Common
Circa: 1867 only
Locale: Benicia, Cal.
Note: This bottle could be listed as rare, but as a long time resident and digger in Benicia, I know of many that have been unearthed. In the Benicia Arsenal 50+ came out of one hole in the early 1970's and I personally have dug over a dozen. The Army probably kept ol Barney McGee in business for the short time he was in Benicia. They have also been dug in Antioch, Napa, San Francisco and no doubt a few other towns on the water. For not being in business very long, his bottles sure got around. He probably used them in San Francisco until his new order was filled for the S.F. location. See bottle below.

HISTORY: *Barney McGee was listed as an attorney and a manufacturer of soda water in the 1867 Pacific Coast Directory. His place of business was on H St. near First. This was the location of John Rueger's Benicia Brewery. It later became the Benicia Steam Soda Works and brewery owned by Rueger's son inlaw Gustave Gnauck.*

Front: B.J. McGEE / SAN FRANCISCO

Round, Smooth Base
Applied Top
Aqua
Green
Ex. Rare
Circa: 1869-1873
Locale: San Francisco
Note: The San Francisco embossed McGee bottle is much more rare than its Benicia counterpart. I know of only one being dug in San Francisco. This was by the longtime digger and soda collector, the late Ken Salazar. A green one was dug in Vallejo and 3 have been dug in Benicia.

HISTORY: *1869-1970 McGee, Barney J., proprietor Union Soda Works, 107 Fifth*
1871-1873 McGee, Barney, Soda Water Manufacturer, 107 Fifth

Front: MISENHEIMER & HALL / ALMA SODA
Base: PACIFIC GLASS WORKS

Round, Smooth Base
Applied Top
Aqua
Ex. Rare
Circa: 1862-1865
Locale: Alma, Cal.
Note: I have not heard of any of these being found in California. One came out of Oregon and 4 were unearthed somewhere in Nevada. It is one of the rarest soda bottles in the West.

HISTORY: *The town of Alma is now under Lexington reservoir in Santa Clara County. Parts of the remains of the town can be seen when the water level is very low. No other info.*

Front: MILLS' / SELTZER / SPRINGS

    Round, Saratoga Shape, Smooth base
    Applied Double Collar Top
    Amber, $5500.00 - 2007, $3600.00 - 200
    Ex. Rare
    Circa: 1874-1885
    Locale: Santa Clara, Cal.

HISTORY: See below bottle.

Front: MILLS' / SELTZER / SPRINGS
Base: M

    Round, Smooth Base
    Applied Top
    Aqua, $150.00 - 2007, $60.00 - 2009
    Scarce
    Varient: Hutch
    Circa: 1874-1885
    Locale: Santa Clara, Cal.

HISTORY: Luther Mills bought the Congress Springs Hotel in 1869, and operated it for five years. After selling out he bought the Seltzer Aperiant Springs in Santa Clara. He developed the springs under the name of Mills Pacific Seltzer Springs and produced mineral water and other products. The springs were later sold to John Ryland, and he ran it under the name of Azule Seltzer Springs.

Front: C MOISE & CO. / SAN FRANCISCO
Re: GENUINE PACIFIC / GINGER BEER

    Round, Smooth Base
    Aqua
    Ex. Rare
    Circa: 1870's (approx.)
    Locale: San Francisco

HISTORY: In 1877 and 1878 Moise was listed as an agent, but does not say what he was an agent for. We assume it was for this soda.

Front: J. MONIER & CO. / CL FR NA
       J. MONIER & CO. / CL FR N

    Round, Iron Pontil
    Applied Top
    Aqua, $350.00 - 2015
    Cobalt, $1100.00 - 2017
    Teal Green, $700.00 - 2010
    Rare
    Circa: 1856-1858
    Locale: San Francisco
    Note: The Monier bottle is found in the S.F. redevelopment areas and the mud flats on the Benicia waterfront. A few have been dug in the early mining camps in Nevada and Placer County, and in Placerville.

HISTORY: Below are the only listings for the years Jerome Monier should have used this bottle.
    1856-1857 Monier & Co., Hair Dressers, 160 ½ Commercial
              Monier, J. of Monier & Constant
    1857-1858 Monier & Co., Hair Dressers, 185 Clay

Front: M. MOONEY / VISALIA

Round, Smooth Base
Applied Top
Aqua, $350.00 - 2021
Blue
Rare
Circa: 1872-1881
Locale: Visalia, Cal.
Note: Found primarily around the Visalia area, one was dug in Suisun City in 1976.
Michael Mooney trade marked this weird drawing for his soda bottles in 1878. See at right.

HISTORY: In 1869 Michael Mooney opened a brewery on the corner of Main and Garden Sts. In June of 1872, Mooney added a soda apparatus to his Brewery business. Then in 1875 he built a new brewery on the corner of Main & Garden. Michael died in 1881 and his brother Hugh Mooney continued operations for some time afterwards.

Front: C MORLEY / VICTORIA / B.C.

Round, Smooth Base
Tooled and Applied Top
Aqua
Rare
Varient: New Westminister instead of Victoria
Hutch, Crown Top, Inside Screw Top
Circa: 1880's, Westminister bottle prior to 1871
Locale: Victoria, B.C., New Westminister, B.C.

HISTORY: Morley's partnership with Greenwood ended in 1879. C. Morley continued on alone until the early 1900's. His place of business remained on Yates St. in Victoria.

Front: MT. TAMALPAIS / NATURAL / MINERAL / WATER CO. / SAN RAFAEL, CAL.
Re: A MILD MINERAL WATER / TAMALPAIS SODA / FREE FROM ALL / DELETERIOUS INGREDIENTS / TRADE MARK

Round, Smooth Base
Tooled Top
Aqua, $1000.00 - 2010,
$550.00 - 2018
Rare
Circa: After 1906
Locale: San Rafael, Cal.

History: The Tamalpais Mineral Well was in San Rafael, Marin County. The well was in the southern part of town in the basement of a building which was then known as the Buffalo Soda Works. New Century and the San Francisco Seltzer Water Co. were the agents, located at 436 Green St. San Francisco.

Front: G.P. / MORRILL

Round, Smooth Base
Applied Top
Aqua, $1000.00 - 2021
Green
Rare
Circa: 1868-1872
Locale: Virginia City, Nevada
Note: Ad at right is circa 1863.

 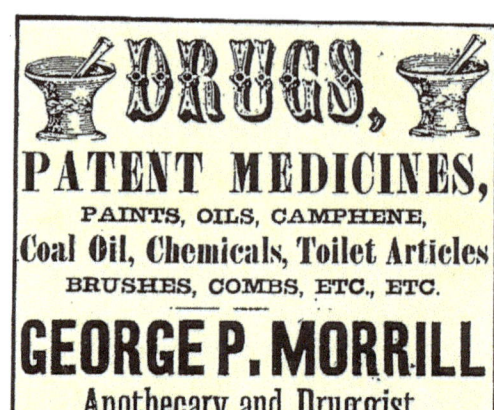

HISTORY: George P. Morrill had a drug store in Placerville, in the early 1860's. Sometime in 1863 he expanded his business to Virginia City, Nevada. He was listed at 16 South C St. and being in the apothecary business. He probably bought W.S. Wright's soda apparatus, and started the soda works in 1868. He was the first Virginia City druggist to bottle his own soda water. Ad at lower left is circa 1868, ad at lower right is circa 1866.

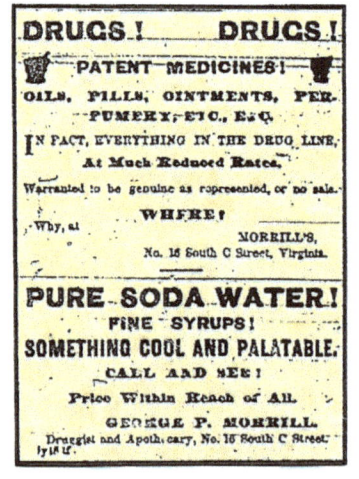   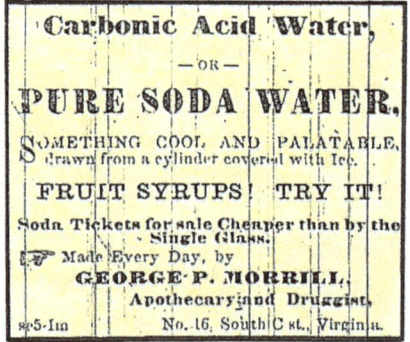

Front: M.R. / SACRAMENTO
Re: UNION GLASS WORKS / PHILADA

Round, Iron Pontil
Applied Top
Cobalt, $2000.00 - 2014
Varient: reverse is blank
Rare
Circa: 1851-1863
Locale: Sacramento, Cal.
Note: In 1861 Martin Rancich applied for a trade mark to identify his bottles. It was for the bases to be painted half white and half green. See application at below right. A blue example came from a ranch site near Woodland.

HISTORY: In the Sacramento City Directory of 1856, it lists Martin Rancich as being established in 1851 with a production of 150 dozen per day.
1851 Martin Rancich, Grocer, 135 J St.
1852-1853 Martin Rancich, Liquor Merchant, 131 J St.
1854-1856 Martin Rancich, Soda Water Manufacturer, 5th near J
1857-1860 Martin Rancich, Soda Water Manufacturer, 5TH between I and J
1861-1863 Martin Rancich, Soda Water Manufacturer, 19 5th St.

Front: M.R. / SACRIMENTO (in slug plate)
Re: UNION GLASS WORKS / PHILADA

Round, Iron Pontil
Applied Top
Green, $1400.00 - 2004
Cobalt
Teal Green, $950.00 - 2007
Rare
Circa: 1851-1863
Locale: Sacramento, Cal.
Note: At least one example was found at the site of Monte Cristo in Sierra Co., and a blue one was dug at a ranch site near Woodland, Cal.
History: See above bottle

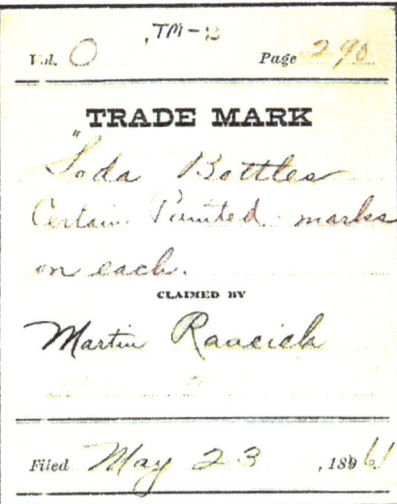

Front: M R & D (in slug plate)
Re: UNION GLASS WORKS / PHILADA

Round, Iron Pontil
Applied Top
Green
Cobalt, $17,000.00 - 2004
Ex. Rare
Circa: 1863-1864
Locale: Sacramento, Cal.
Note: One of these Ex. Rare sodas was found at a ranch site near Davis, Cal. in the 1990's, and another was found near Cedarville in El Dorado County.

HISTORY: Gaetano Deluchi worked for Martin Rancich in his soda factory in the early 1850's. In 1863 Rancich took Deluchi on as a partner in his soda water business. After 1864 neither Rancich or Deluchi were listed in the soda or mineral water business again. Martin Rancich pops up in 1871 as the proprietor of the Central Rest. on K St. Deluchi became a commission merchant in Sacramento.

Front: NAPA / SODA
Re: HAAS BROS. / NATURAL / MINERAL WATER

Round, Smooth Base
Applied Top
Aqua
Lime Green
Cobalt, $550.00 - 2021
Scarce in Blue and Aqua
Ex. Rare in Green
Circa: 1873-1877
Locale: Napa, Cal.

HISTORY: David L. Haas applied for a trade mark for this bottle in 1873. I do not believe this bottle was in use for very long after 1873, because Col. Jackson took over the Napa Soda Springs and the bottles were embossed Jackson's Napa Soda at that point. However there is a listing for 1875-1876 that states that the Haas Bros. were agents for the Napa Soda Depot in Napa. The Haas Bros. were probably the agents for Napa Soda Water for Napa Co. before M. Silva.

Front: NAPA / SODA
Re: NATURAL / MINERAL WATER
Base: W (on some)

Round, Smooth Base
Applied Top
Amber, Aqua
Green, $550.00 - 2009
Lt. Green, $300.00 - 2019
Cobalt, $550.00 - 2021
Med. Blue, $190.00 - 2021
Scarce
Ex. Rare in Amber
Varient: Different Fonts
Circa: 1861-1873
Locale: San Francisco
Note: These bottles sometimes have heavy case wear that greatly affects their value.

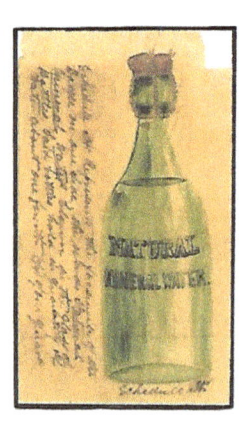

HISTORY: Bottles with this embossing were discontinued in 1873 when Col Jackson assumed ownership of the springs. Its possible that J.H. Wood used the bottles with the W on the base. J. Henry Wood applied for a patent in 1864 for this embossing pattern. See drawing above.

Front: NAPA / SODA
Re: NATURAL / MINERAL WATER / T.A.W.

Round, Smooth Base
Applied Top
Teal Green, $650.00 - 2012, $275.00 - 2021
Teal Blue
Rare
Circa: 1861-1862
Locale: San Francisco
Note: One was dug in the Wilmington District in Fremont and another in Suisun City.

HISTORY: 1861 White, Thomas A., Napa Springs
              Importer, Office 521 Washington
           1862 White, Thomas A., agent Napa
              Mineral Waters, 613 Sansome
           1862 was the first year Napa Soda Springs
              was listed in San Francisco. Ad circa 1861.

Front: NAPA / SODA / B.F. CONNOLLY
Re: NATURAL / MINERAL WATER

Round, Smooth Base
Applied Top
Aqua, $350.00 - 2021
Rare
Circa: 1872-1873
Locale: Petaluma, Cal.

History: B.F. Connolly was the agent for Napa Soda in Sonoma Co.
        in the early 1870's. This was company previously known as
        Connolly & Bro.

Front: NAPA / SODA / PHIL CADUC
Re: NATURAL / MINERAL WATER

Round, Smooth Base
Applied Top
Aqua, $100.00 - 2021
Lime Green, $325.00 - 2009
Deep Teal Green,
* $300.00 - 2010*
Cobalt, $550.00 - 2019
Med. Blue, $230.00 - 2021
Green, $160.00 - 2019
Common in Aqua
Rare in Colors
Circa: 1873-1881
Locale: Sacramento, Cal.

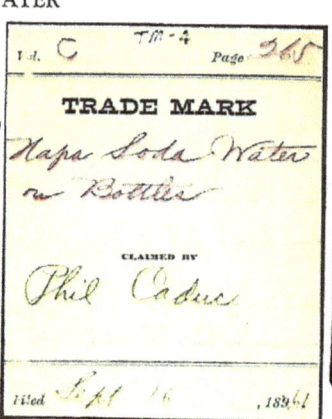

HISTORY: Phil Caduc was the agent for Napa Soda in Sacramento as early as 1861. He probably used the bottles that were marked with just Napa Soda on the front. See trade mark above. In 1873 when Col. Jackson took over the Napa Soda Springs, that forced Phil Caduc to have a new bottle made with his name on it.

1873-1874 Caduc, Phil, agent for Napa Soda, Pacific
            Congress Water, 41-47 3rd between J & K
1874-1879 Caduc, Phil, agent for Philadelphia Brewery, Napa Soda and Pacific
            Congress Water, 41-47 3rd between J & K
1879-1880 Caduc, Phil, Agent Napa Soda, ale and porter and dealer in coal, 41-47 3RD
1880-1881 Caduc, Phil, Agent for Napa Soda Water and dealer in coal, 1009-1015 3rd
In 1881 Louis Leloy took over as the agent for Napa Soda Water in Sacramento.

Front: NAPA / SODA / LOUIS LELOY
Re: NATURAL / MINERAL WATER

Round, Smooth Base
Applied Top
Aqua, $90.00 - 2021
Scarce
Circa: 1881-1884
Locale: Sacramento, Cal.

HISTORY: In 1881 Louis Leloy took over as the agent for Napa Soda in Sacramento from Phil Caduc.
    1880-1881 Leloy, Louis, Hairdresser, Liquors and Cigars, 224 J St.
    1881-1884 Leloy, Louis, Liquors and Cigars, 222 J St.
                Leloy, Louis, Soda and Mineral Water, 228 J St.

Front: NAPA / SODA / P & W SF
Re: NATURAL / MINERAL WATER

Round, Open Pontil
Applied Top
Green
Ex. Rare, No Known Whole Specimens
Circa: Late 1850's - Early 1860's
Locale: San Francisco
Note: The size of the Letters and Font is much different than
*   the other Napa Soda bottles listed here.*

Front: NAPA / SODA / W & W SF
Re: NATURAL / MINERAL WATER

    Round, Smooth Base
    Applied Top
    Green
    Ex. Rare (no whole specimens known)
    Circa: 1860's
    Locale: San Francisco

HISTORY: No info at this time.

Front: NAPA / 'STAR' / WOOD'S / 'STAR' / SODA
Re: NATURAL / MINERAL / WATER / T.W.F. A.G.T.

    Round, Smooth Base
    Applied Top
    Cobalt, $1200.00 - 2019, $900.00 - 2021
    Green
    Rare
    Circa: 1870-1872
    Locale: San Francisco

HISTORY: 1870 Napa Soda Company, office 111 Post
              Fenn, Thomas W., Natural Soda Water, 111 Post
        1871 Napa Soda Company, Thomas W. Fenn, Agent
              Office, 124 Sutter
        1872, Napa, Soda, Fenn & Burdell Agents, Office
              124 Sutter

Front: NEYMAN & DRAKE (block letters around body) / MOK HILL / UNION GLASS WORKS
Re: PHILADA

    Round, Iron Pontil
    Applied Top
    Teal Blue, $1400.00 - 2004
    Ex. Rare
    Circa: 1850's
    Locale: Mokelumne Hill, Cal.
    Note: Rumor has it that most of the known specimens of this bottle were found in one hole in Stcockton in the late 1960's. or '70s

HISTORY: No info at this time

Front: NEVADA CITY / SODA WORKS / L. SIEBERT

    Round, Smooth Base
    Applied Top
    Green
    Aqua, $300.00 - 2021
    Scarce
    Circa: 1870's to early 1880's
    Locale: Nevada City, Cal.
    Note: These are commonly found in the Nevada City, Grass Valley area, with a lime green specimen coming out of Grass Valley.

HISTORY: Not much is known about Louis Seibert in the soda water business other than in the early 1880's he is listed as a soda water manufacturer in Nevada City. The 1880 Thompson & West atlas of Nevada Co. has a litho showing his soda works and vineyard. See next page.

Front: NEW ALMADEN
Re: MINERAL WATER / W & W

    10 Sided, Iron Pontil
    Applied Top
    Aqua
    Green
    Ex. Rare
    Circa: 1854-1860 (approx.)
    Locale: San Jose, Cal.

HISTORY: *Thomas and David Williams were bottling water from the springs at the New Almaden Mines in 1854, when they moved into the city of San Jose. They bought the apparatus of Gerriche and Leach, who had the first soda water bottling house in the city, and commenced the manufacturing of soda water. This was on St. John, between First and Market. From the spring of 1854, they bottled about 100 dozen per day, which later increased to 3 times that amount.*

The Williams Brothers also had a partner in this venture by the name of Winslow. Prior to 1872 the company was listed as Winslow and Williams. This would account for the embossing of W & W on the bottles. A trade mark was applied for in 1863 by Williams and Winslow for this embossing pattern. See drawing. This was for the bottle below.

Front: NEW ALMADEN / MINL WATER
Re: 1870 / W & W (block letters)

    Round, Smooth Base
    Applied Top
    Aqua, $350.00 - 2021
    Blue
    Common in Aqua
    Ex. Rare in Blue
    Variant: "1870" on front
    Circa: 1860-1872
    Locale: San Jose, Cal.

HISTORY: *See above bottle*

Front: NEW ALMADEN / VICHY WATER / CALIFORNIA
Re: TRADE 'CREST' MARK / A.P.

    Round, with Footed Smooth Base
    Applied Top
    Aqua, $3600.00 - 2005
    Ex. Rare
    Circa: 1870-1874
    Locale: San Francisco
    Note: 2 of these rare bottles have been found in Suisun City and 2 in San Francisco.

HISTORY: *The New Almaden Vichy Springs were near the New Almaden Mines in Santa Clara Co. The springs went dry around 1880, due to the workings of the Quicksilver Mines nearby.*

    1871-1872 New Almaden Vichy Water, O. Chauvin Agent, Office 506 Jackson
    1872-1874 Chauvin, Onesime, agent New Almaden Vichy Water Co., Office 607 Washington

F.L.A. Pioche applied for a trade mark for this bottle in 1869. His initials would explain the A.P. on the bottle.

Front: TRADE / 'monogram' / MARK / A.P. / NEW ALMADEN / VICHY WATER / CALIFORNIA

Round, Smooth Base
13" Tall, Quart, 10" tall, Pint
Applied Top
Green, Pint, $2800.00 - 2008
Olive Amber, Pint
Yellow Green, Quart, $3200.00 - 2008
Teal Green, Quart, $3000.00 - 2010
Amber, Quart, $1500.00 - 2010 (flake)
Deep Aqua, Quart
Note: Label trade marked in 1869 by
       Francis L.A. Pioche in S.F.
Pints are to the right
Quarts are below
Note: These bottles are found in many towns in
   the San Francisco bay area. From San Jose to
   the south to Santa Rosa, Vallejo, Suisun City and
   Fairfield.

HISTORY: See previous bottle.

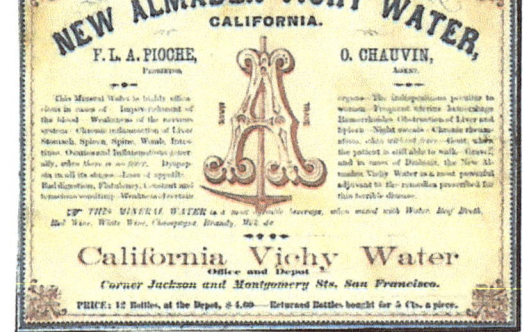

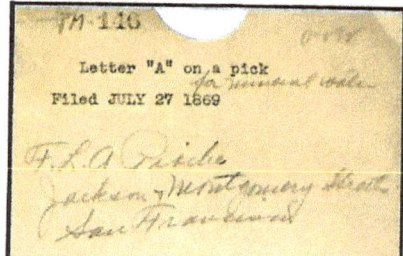

65

Front: NEW CENTURY / MINERAL / WATER
Base: P C G W

Round, Smooth Base
Tooled Top
Aqua
Rare
Varient; Hutch and Crown Top
Circa: 1904-1910
Locale: San Francisco

HISTORY: 1904 New Century Soda Works, Puccinelli & Belli Proprietors, 713 Laguna
1905 New Century Steam Soda Works, Puccinelli & Belli Proprietors, 713 Union
1906 New Century Soda Works, 3125 Laguna
1907 New Century Soda Water Company, 3125 Laguna
1908 New Century Soda Works Company, 3209 Laguna
1909 New Century Soda Works Company, 439 Green
1910 Company changed name to San Francisco and New Century Seltzer Co.

Front: NEW LIBERTY S.W. CO. / TRADE 'MAN' MARK / S.F. (in round plate)

Round, Smooth Base
Aqua
Rare
Varient: Hutch
Circa: 1899-1902
Locale: San Francisco

HISTORY: 1899-1900 New Liberty Soda Water Co., H. Schmidt & Co. Proprietor, 3272 24th
1900-1902 New Liberty Soda Works, Herman Schmidt Proprietor, 3272 24th

---

Front: NONPAREIL / SODA WATER CO. / S.F.
Base: B B B

Round, Smooth base
Tooled and Applied Top
Aqua, Tooled Top, $250.00 - 2017
Lime Green, Applied Top, $500.00 - 2017
Rare with Applied Top
Scarce with Tooled Top
Circa: 1881-1887
Locale: San Francisco

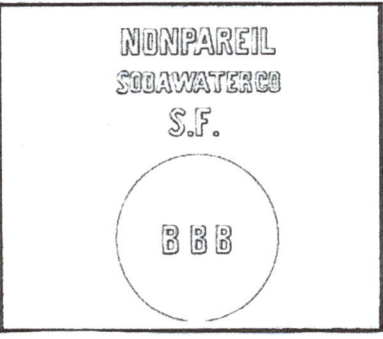

HISTORY: Samuel Benjamin was the proprietor of the Nonpareil Soda Water Co. from 1881-1887. It was located at 719-721 Bryant. Prior to 1881 the Eastern Cider Co. was located at this address. J.P. Benjamin of S.F. applied for a trade mark for this brand in 1886. See drawing above.

Base: PACIFIC GLASS WORKS

Round, Smooth Base
Applied Top
Teal Blue, $650.00 - 2017
Green, $1500.00 - 2017
Aqua, $140.00 - 2019
Rare in all colors
Circa: 1863-1876
Locale: San Francisco
Note: Ad circa 1872. An aqua example was dug in Grass Valley in the 1990's.

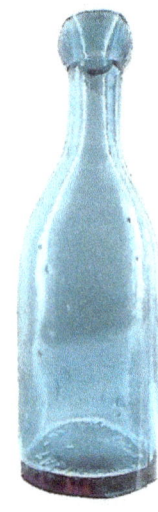

HISTORY: Warren Friedrich's book on early California Glass Works covers the history more completely than I could ever do here. I highly recommend it.

1863-1864 Pacific Glass Works, cor Iowa and Mariposa, Potrero, office 514 Washington

1865-1866 Pacific Glass Works, Mariposa nr Mississippi, Potrero, office 621 Clay

1867-1874 Pacific Glass Works, Bennett & Co. proprietors, cor Iowa and Mariposa, New Potrero, office 514 Washington

1875-1876 Pacific Glass Works, John Taylor and R.K. Pattridge, works corner Iowa and Mariposa, Potrero, John Taylor & Co. agents, office 514 Washington

1876 The San Francisco Glass Works and the Pacific Glass Works joined forces and the company was then known as the San Francisco and Pacific Glass Works.

Front: PACIFIC / CONGRESS / WATER
Re: PHIL CADUC

Round, Smooth Base
Applied Top
Aqua, $100.00 - 2021
Scarce
Circa: 1868-1881
Locale: Sacramento, Cal.

HISTORY: See Napa Soda / Phil Caduc

Front: PACIFIC CONGRESS WATER

Round, Smooth Base
Applied Top
Aqua, $50.00 - 2010
Green, $1100.00 - 2021
Cobalt, $750.00 - 2008
Teal Blue, $180.00 - 2007 (crack)
Blue, $2000.00 - 2021
Common in Aqua
Rare in Shades of Green and Blue
Ex. Rare in Cobalt
Circa: 1869-1876
Locale: San Francisco
Note: A blue one was dug in Benicia in 1977.

HISTORY: See Pacific Congreess Water next page

Front: PACIFIC CONGRESS / WATER
Re: 'RUNNING DEER'

Round, Smooth Base
Applied and Tooled Top
Aqua, A.T., $50.00 - 2010
Aqua, T.T., $325.00 - 2021
Green, $180.00 - 2009
Circa: 1869-1876
Locale: San Francisco
Common in Aqua
Rare in Green

HISTORY: *From 1869 to 1874 this bottle was used by Luther R. Mills, who was the owner of the Pacific Congress Springs Depot in S.F. during these years. From 1874 to 1875 Louis A. Sage used this bottle and had his name embossed on it. Henry A. Benjamin and Co. were the pro-prietors of the Pacific Congress Springs from 1875 thru 1880. He may have used this bottle for a short time, which would account for the bottles with the Sage name being slugged out.*

Front: PACIFIC CONGRESS / SPRINGS

Round, Smooth Base
Applied Double Collar and Blob Top
Saratoga Shape
Cobalt: $7000.00 - 2008
Lt. Blue, $2000.00 - 2021
Green, $800.00 - 2008 (bruise)
Ex. Rare
Circa: Late 1860's to 1870's
Locale: San Francisco

HISTORY: *See above bottle*

Front: PACIFIC CONGRESS WATER SPRINGS SARATOGA /
       'DEER' / CALIFORNIA
Re   PACIFIC CONGRESS / SPRINGS

Round, Smooth Base
Applied Double Collar Top
Saratoga Shape
Teal Green, $4400.00 - 2017
Olive Amber, $4000.00 - 2009
Olive Green, $4000.00 - 2021
Green, $1100.00 - 2021 (repaired)
Rare
Circa: 1870's
Locale: San Francisco

Front: PACIFIC CONGRESS WATER SPRINGS SARATOGA / 'DEER' / CALIFORNIA
Re: SAGE'S / PACIFIC CONGRESS / SPRINGS

Round, Smooth Base
Applied Double Collar Top
Saratoga Shape
Lime Green, $3200.00 - 2021
Yellow Green, $3000.00 - 2012
Grass Green, $5000.00 - 2021
Ex. Rare
Circa: 1874-1875
Locale: San Francisco
Note: Ad below is circa 1875.

HISTORY: See previous 3 bottles

PACIFIC Congress Spring,
SARATOGA,
ONLY TWELVE MILES FROM SAN JOSE.

LEWIS P. SAGE, Prop'r.

MINERAL BATHS,
HOT AND COLD.

This institution has been established about eight years, and under its present proprietorship is fast gaining a reputation of which it may justly feel proud.

Front: PACIFIC / SODA / WORKS
Re: SAN / FRANCISCO

Round, Smooth Base
Applied Top
Green
Aqua, $130.00 - 2017
Rare
Circa: 1868-1870
Locale: San Francisco

HISTORY: 1868-69 Pacific Soda Works, John F. Rohe, proprietor, 115 Jessie
1869-70 Pacific Soda Works, John F. Rohe, proprietor, 1112 Market
The Pacific Soda Works was established in 1853 by D.A. Mowry. It was located on the corner of Jessie and Jane. The soda works retained it's name until 1870 under various owners, including James Classen who had his name embossed on the bottles. See Classen.

Front: F. PAILLET / NATURAL / MINERAL / WATER / S.F.
Re: NATURAL / MINERAL WATER / FROM THE / GOLDEN WEST SPRINGS / NAPA / COUNTY CAL.

Round, Smooth Base
Tooled Top
Aqua
Rare
Circa: 1901-1906
Locale: San Francisco

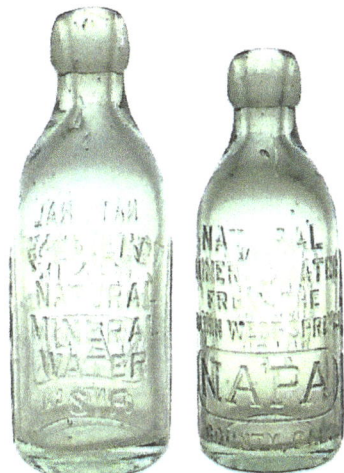

HISTORY: 1901-1902 Paillet, Frank, Soda Water Works, 820 Buchanan
Golden West Soda Works, 820 Buchanan
1903-1906 Paillet, Frank, proprietor Golden West Soda Works, 1619 Farrell
In 1901 Peter Somps took over the Golden West Soda Works which was owned by Frank Paillet and P. Somps. It was located at 624 Laguna at the time. That forced Paillet to look for a new location to carry on his business. This bottle is the same bottle used by Herve and Somps. See E. Herve and P. Somps.

Front: T. PARSONS / SALT LAKE CITY

Round, Smooth Base
Applied Top
Aqua
Ex. Rare
Circa: 1880's
Locale: Salt Lake City, Utah

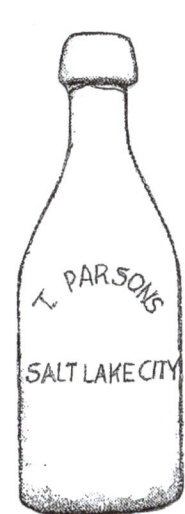

HISTORY: Thomas Parsons was the proprietor of the Salt Lake City Bottling House and Soda Factory on Commercial St. during the early 1880's. The Parsons bottles are territorial bottles being that Utah did not become a state until 1896.

Front: T. PARSONS / SALT LAKE CITY / UTAH

Round, Smooth Base
Applied Top
Aqua
Rare
Circa: 1880's
Locale: Salt Lake City, Utah
Note: Ad at right circa 1881.

HISTORY: See above bottle

Front: P. & B. / COLUSA, / CAL.

Round, Smooth Base
Applied Top
Aqua, $325.00 - 2009
Rare
Circa: 1887-1888
Locale: Colusa, Cal.
Note: Most of the known specimens of this bottle were found in privys in Colusa.

HISTORY: The Colusa Soda Works was started in 1877 by J.L. Poulson. It was on the corner of 3rd and Market Sts. In 1878 Poulson had to rebuild the soda works after a fire. He operated it alone until April of 1885, at which time he sold out to T.H. Polly. Polly was the sole proprietor until late 1887, when he added Rankin Blackburn as a partner. This lasted only until 1888 when R. Blackburn was listed as the sole proprietor. Blackburn retained ownership until after 1900 when he sold the soda works to T.F. Phillips.

Front: PEARSON'S / SODA WORKS

Round, Smooth Base
Applied Top
Aqua, $250.00 - 2021
Scarce
Varient: Hutch and a Wide Mouth Bottle
Circa: 1870's
Locale: Placerville, Cal.

HISTORY: John Pearson established the Pearson Soda Works in 1852. In 1890 John Sr. passed away and John Pearson Jr. took over the business, and expanded it by distributing beer, wine, cider and liquor as well as soda water. John Jr. died in 1917 and his wife carried on until 1920, when she sold the business of the Placerville Soda Works to the Scheerer Bros. The Scheerer Bros. also held the local Coca Cola franchise but had not thought enough of it to produce any product. In 1936 R.A. Hook bought out the Scheerer Bros and immediately expanded the business to produce the now famous Coca Cola soda. The blob top bottle considered here should date from the mid 1870's to early 1880's.

A bit more on the Pearson Bros., in 1876 they started a soda works in Carson City, Nevada. It was located on South Carson St at 5th. It was closed in 1881 by two lawsuits. In 1880 they had ventured to Bodie, Cal. and opened a soda works there. It was sold in 1883, and they returned to Placerville. The blob top bottle shown here has been found in all three locations., as well as Georgetown, Cal. They also used a gravitator type bottle in Bodie, and it is the only one with a town embossed on it.

Front: PHILLIP'S / NAPA / MINERAL WATER
Re: PHILLIP'S / NAPA / MINERAL WATER

Round, Smooth Base
Tooled Top
Aqua
Common
Circa: 1899-1901
Locale: San Francisco

HISTORY: 1898 See Walters Napa County Soda
1899 *Phillip's Napa County Soda Company, (formerly Walters), S.A. Phillips manager, 717 McAllister, Tel Mint 1481*
1900 *Phillip's Napa County Soda Company (inc.), 2037 15th, Samuel A. Phillips*
1901 *Popular Soda Water Company, (S.A. Phillips & I.H. Spiro) 2037 15th*

Front: PHILLIPS / NAPA / CO. / SODA
Re: PHILLIPS / SODA SPRINGS / NATURAL / MINERAL WATER

Round, Smooth Base
Tooled Top
Aqua
Scarce
Varient: Crown Top
Circa: 1899-1901
Locale: San Francisco

HISTORY: See above bottle

Front: PIONEER / 'BEAR' / SODA WATER CO. / S.F.
Re: CLUB SODA (embossed diagonally)

Round, Smooth Base
Applied Top
Aqua
Rare
Variant: Hutch and Crown Top
Circa: 1897-1906
Locale: San Francisco

HISTORY: Prior to 1897 this company was known as the Pioneer Soda Water Works. Martin Walsh and Charles Welch were the proprietors. The name change to the Pioneer Soda Water Company occurred in 1897. The proprietors at this time were William Welch and George Collins. They were located at 1555 Mission St. This partnership lasted until 1902, when the Soda Company was sold to Louis Thierback. He operated it until 1906.

Front: PIONEER / BROWN & CO.

Round, Smooth Base
Applied Top
Blue
Green, $2800.00 - 2021
Aqua
Ex. Rare
Circa: 1866-1870
Locale: Idaho City, Idaho, 1866-1869
        Hamilton, Nevada, 1869-1870

F. C. BROWN & CO.,
Pioneer Soda Water Factory,
HAMILTON, NEVADA.
ARE READY TO SERVE CUSTOMERS IN THIS and surrounding Districts.   je16-1m

HISTORY: Langley's Pacific Coast Directory lists F. Brown & Co. as the proprietors of the Pioneer Soda Works in Idaho City, Idaho in 1867. This was no doubt the first soda works in the Idaho Territory. Sometime in early 1869 he decided to move his business to Hamilton, Nevada, another isolated mining camp. He started advertising in the White Pine News. in mid 1869. Ad above is from 1869. These bottles have been found in Silver City and Idaho City in Idaho, as well as in Treasure City, Hamilton and Virginia City in Nevada, and even as far west as Marin Co., Cal.

Front: PIONEER SODA WORKS / SAN FRANCISCO
Base: T

Round, Smooth Base
Applied Top
Aqua
Common
Circa: 1866-1873
Locale: San Francisco
Note: Embossing pattern was trade marked on Oct. 18, 1862 by C. Turner Jr. and J.E. Fitzpatrick. See at right. These have been dug in Dutch Flat and Grass Valley.

PIONEER SODA WORKS
SAN FRANCISCO

HISTORY: The first listing for the Pioneer Soda Works was in 1854. With Cephus Turner & Co. (John Fitzpatrick) being the proprietors. They were located at the rear of 280 Dupont St. In 1858 Turner added Peter Brader as a partner. This lasted until 1860. In 1860 Turner and John Rohe were now listed as proprietors. From 1863 thru 1865, Fitzpatrick and James Bliven were listed as proprietors, at 529 Jackson St.. Then from 1866 until 1872, Turner and Fitzpatrick were again listed as the proprietors. After 1872 they went to work for the Bay City Soda Water Co.

Front: PIONEER / SODA WORKS / PSW (in a shield) / SAN FRANCISCO

>Round, Smooth Base
>Applied and Tooled Top
>Aqua, $180.00 - 2010
>Rare
>Circa: 1877-1896
>Locale: San Francisco

HISTORY: Martin Walsh, Charles Welch and Raymo Angelo were the proprietors of the Pioneer Soda Works from 1877 thru 1883. They were located at 1719 ½ Market St, then moving to 1721 Market St. in 1881. In 1884 Angelo is no longer listed as a partner. From 1884-1895 Walsh and Welch were the proprietors, remaining at the 1721 Market St. address. In 1896 they moved to 1555 Mission where they continued until taken over by Wm. Welch and George Collins in 1897.
There was also a Pioneer Soda Works located at 21 and 22 Hinckley from 1878 until 1882. This was owned by Henry Wiggett and Charles Lupton. They were listed as manufacturers of ginger beer and soda water. It is not known if they used any of these Pioneer bottles.

Front: PIONEER / SODA WORKS / TRADE 'SHIELD' MARK / S.F.

>Round, Smooth Base
>Applied and Tooled Top
>Aqua, Applied Top, $140.00 - 2021
>Lt. Green, Applied Top, $210.00 - 2017
>Blue
>Common in Aqua
>Scarce in Colors
>Varient: without "S.F.", with "W" in shield
>Circa: 1877-1896
>Locale: San Francisco

HISTORY: See above bottle. Welch and Walsh applied for a trade mark in 1886, see drawing above.

Front: PORTLAND / TRADE MARK / "EAGLE" / SODA WORKS / P.O.

>Round, Smooth Base
>Applied Top
>Aqua, $275.00 - 2021
>Rare
>Varient: Hutch
>Circa: 1880's
>Locale: Portland, Oregon

HISTORY: From 1883-1911, Frank Northrup and George Sturgis were the proprietors of the Portland Soda Works. They were located at 93-95 Oak St. in Portland. They advertised that their factory was the largest, oldest and best establishment of its kind in the Pacific Northwest.

Front: E.A. POST / 'EAGLE' / PORTLAND OGN

Round, Smooth Base
Applied Top
Aqua
Lt. Teal
Rare
Circa: 1881-1883 (approx)
Locale: Portland, Oregon

HISTORY: Edward A. Post was listed as being the sole proprietor of the Portland Soda Works, for only one year, that being 1882. It was located at 146 Front St. between Alder and Morrison.

Front: PRIEST / NAPA
Re: NATURAL / BOTTLED / AT THE / SPRINGS / MINERAL WATER

Round, Smooth Base
Tooled Top
Aqua
Ex. Rare
Circa: 1883-1906
Locale: Napa, Cal.

HISTORY: The Priest Soda Springs were located in a canyon of the same name in Napa County. J.J. Priest operated the bottling establishment until his death in 1897. A son, D.C. Priest, continued to bottle water at the springs with another brother. In later years they operated a bottling works in St. Helena, Cal.

Front: PRIEST'S / NATURAL / SODA
Re: NATURAL / 'MAN' / MINERAL WATER

Round, Smooth Base
Applied Top
Lime Green
Aqua, $40.00 - 2010
Scarce
Circa: 1883-1906
Locale: Napa, Cal.

HISTORY: See above bottle

Front: PRIEST / SODA
Re: NATURAL / "MAN" / MINERAL WATER

Round, Smooth Base
Tooled Top
Aqua
Scarce
Variant: the word "SODA" is in a straight line
Circa: 1883-1906
Locale: Napa, Cal.

HISTORY: See above bottles.

Front: PRIEST / NAPA / VALLEY / SODA
Re: NATURAL / MINERAL WATER / RECARBONATED / FROM / NAPA / VALLEY CAL / THIS BOTTLE NEVER / SOLD

Round, Smooth Base
Tooled Top
Aqua
Common
Varient: Crown Top
Circa: 1883-1906
Locale: Napa, Cal.

HISTORY: See previous page

Front: PRIEST / NATURAL / SODA
Re: NATURAL MINERAL WATER / PRIEST / BOTTLED AT THE SPRINGS

Round, Smooth Base
Tooled Top
Aqua
Common
Varient: reverse has: NATURAL / BOTTLED / AT THE
    SPRINGS / MINERAL WATER
Circa: 1883-1906
Locale: Napa, Cal.

HISTORY: See previous page

Front: R & H / COLUMBIA / CAL.

Round, Iron Pontil
Applied Top
Aqua
Lt. Teal Green, $6000.00 - 2017
Ex. Rare
Circa: 1852-1856
Locale: Columbia, Cal.

HISTORY: In 1852 Victor R. Raymond joined A.S. and C.C. Horton in the soda water manufacturing business. The spring was in nearby Gold Springs, and they continued this venture until 1856. No other info at this time. The town site of Columbia is now a California State Historic Park with many Gold Rush era buildings still standing.

Front: C.A. REINERS & CO. / 723 TURK ST / S.F.
Re: IMPROVED / TRADE MARK / 'MOON & STARS' / MINERAL WATER

Round, Smooth Base
Applied Top
Aqua, $100.00 - 2021
Lime Green, $750.00 - 2017
Aqua Green, $220.00 - 2021
Common in Aqua
Rare in Green
Variant: Hutch
Circa: 1875-1882
Locale: San Francisco
Note: Reiners bottles are known to be found in many bay area towns, including Vallejo, Benicia, Pacheco and Napa. A few have even come out of the Gold Country in Grass Valley.

HISTORY: C.A. Reiners was first listed in the soda water trade in 1872. He was in partnership with John Breig as the proprietors of the Eureka Soda Works. Their place of business was listed at 541 and 543 Bryant St. This lasted until 1875 at which time Reiners moved the business to 723 Turk St. That's when this bottle went in use. The trade mark above was applied for in 1873 by C.A. Reiners. Notice the shape of the "R" in the drawing. They have the famous curved leg like so many bottles that were blown in S.F. during this period. Maybe the mold maker was following the patent drawing precisely when he came up with the idea of the curved leg "R". He must have thought it looked good and kept on using it. Just a thought.

Front: C.A. REINERS & CO. / SAN FRANCISCO
Re: IMPROVED / TRADE MARK / 'MOON & STARS' / MINERAL WATER

Round, Smooth Base
Applied Top
Aqua, $500.00 - 2014, $375.00 - 2021
Rare
Circa: 1873-1875
Locale: San Francisco

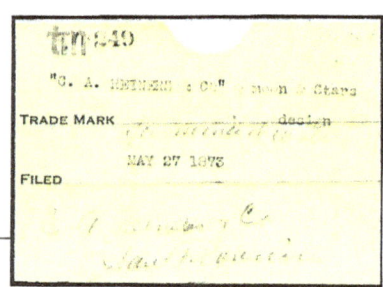

HISTORY: See above bottle

Front: SAGE'S / PACIFIC CONGRESS / WATER
Re: 'DEER'

Round, Smooth Base
Applied and Tooled top
Aqua, $200.00 - 2010, $350.00 - 2009
Rare
Varient: Sage's is slugged out
    Green, $350.00 - 2009
Circa: 1874-1875
Locale: San Francisco

HISTORY: See Pacific Congress Water
    1874-75 Louis Sage & Co. (Henry W. Klein) agent for Pacific Congress Water, 162 Montgomery

Front: SAMUEL'S / NAPA / SODA / SPRINGS
Re: NATURAL / MINERAL WATER / A & B
Base: M

Round, Smooth Base
Applied and Tooled Top
Aqua
Varient: "C" on base
          Minus the "A & B"
Common in all varients
Circa: 1886-1906
Locale: Napa, Cal.

HISTORY: Samuel Springs was located in Napa County and originally founded by E.C. Samuels in the late 1870's. It was located on the western edge on what now is Lake Berryessa. There are many varients and agents of this brand. Here are most if not all of them. Initials on the front and base, such as A in a square, A in a triangle, M in a triangle with S & O on base, M in a triangle with E.S. on base, M in a triangle with M on base, G in a triangle with G on base, etc. Some of these initials are a guess, but we believe the A was for W.F. Alexander, who applied for a trade mark for Samuels Napa Soda in 1886. The E.S. is for E.C. Samuels who was the owner of the springs. The G stood for George H. Gregory, who was the sole agent for San Joaquin County in the 1890's, and was located at 239 East Market in Stockton, Cal. William Brown also trade marked this brand in 1887, with the A and B on the reverse. See drawing. Maybe this was for Alexander and Brown. A J.R. Morris also applied for a trade mark in 1897, this closely resembles the bottle embossing on the newer varients. Morris was from Monticello, the closest town to the springs. It is now under Lake Berryessa. George Gardner, from Napa, also applied for a trade mark in 1887. This would account for the G on some bottles.

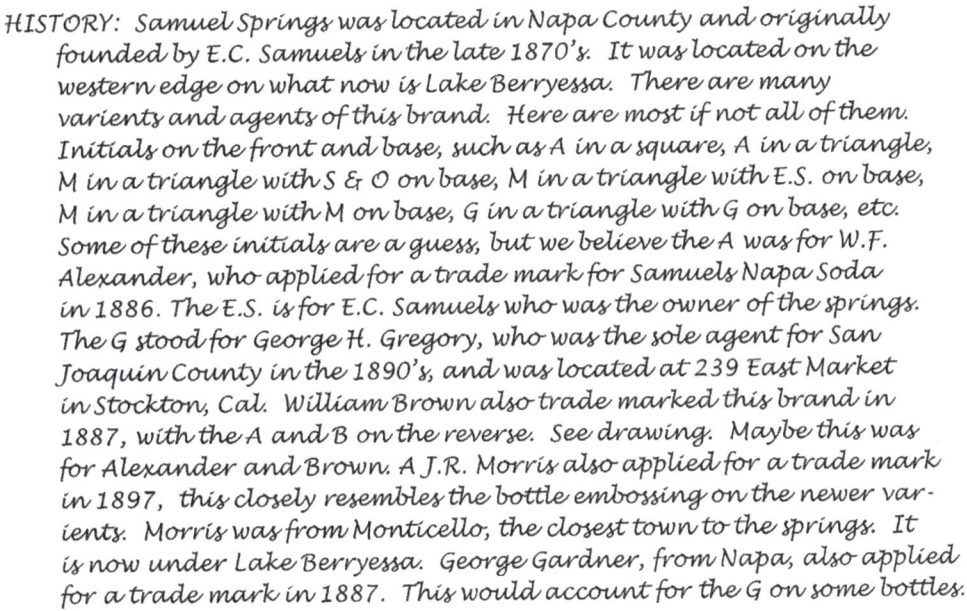

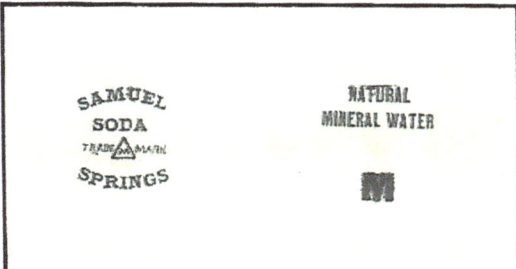

Front: SAMUEL'S / NAPA / SPRINGS
Re: NATURAL / MINERAL WATER

   Round, Smooth Base
   Applied and Tooled Top
   Aqua
   Common
   Varient: "TRADE MARK" under Napa
   Circa: 1886-1906
   Locale: Napa, Cal.

HISTORY: See previous bottle

Front: SAMUEL / SODA / TRADE 'TRIANGLE' MARK / SPRINGS
Re: NATURAL / MINERAL WATER

   Round, Smooth Base
   Tooled Top
   Aqua, Lime Green
   Common in Aqua
   Rare in Green
   Varient: Different Letters in the Triangle
            Crown Top, Amber and Aqua
            Quart Crown Top, Aqua
   Circa: 1890's – 1906
   Locale: Napa, Cal.

History: See previous two bottles

Front: SAN RAFAEL / SODA WORKS / J. KAPPENMAN / PROP'T

   Round, Smooth Base
   Applied Top
   Aqua, $1200.00 - 2018
   Ex. Rare
   Circa: 1879-1880
   Locale: San Rafael, Cal.

HISTORY: Joseph Kappenman was the proprietor of the San Rafael
   Soda Works. This was San Rafael's first soda works and was in
   business from 1879-1880, located at Fourth and H Sts.

Front: SAN RAFAEL / SODA WORKS / P & B / PROP'T'S

   Round, Smooth Base
   Applied Top
   Aqua, $2400.00 - 2009
   Ex. Rare
   Circa: 1880-1885 (approx)
   Locale: San Rafael, Cal.

History: Alphone Bresson and Sylvan Provencal took over the soda works
   from Joseph Kappenman sometime in 1880. Seems they used the same
   bottle, just reworked the mold to suit them.

Front: SAN FRANCISCO / GLASS WORKS

Round, Smooth Base
Applied Top
Greenish Aqua, $170.00 - 2019
Cobalt, $500.00 - 2009, $850.00 - 2007
Deep Aqua, $550.00 - 2019
Aqua, $100.00 - 2021
Aqua with Green Streaks, $220.00 - 2021
Common in shades of Aqua
Rare in Colors
Circa: 1870-1876
Locale: San Francisco
Note: This bottle has been found in many places as any soda company could have used them. Vallejo has yielded dark green and blue examples, one was found in Anaheim, and even as far away as Salt Lake City. Two green ones were dug in Dutch Flat in the mid 1990's.

HISTORY: For a complete and detailed history please see Warren Friedrich's book on Early California Glass Houses. Here is an overview in 1872. Carleton Newman and Duval were the proprietors, with the factory located near the foot of Fourth St. A large building has been built fot the manufacture of the common articles of glass. Demijohns, carboys, pickle, wine, spice, soda, medicine bottles, window glass, etc, were some of the items blown here. The building was 78' by 67' and built out of wood and iron on a brick basement. Its cost was around $20,000.00. The factory is capable of producing about $350.00 per day of products, and employs up to 40 workmen.

1870 San Francisco Glass Works, S Side Townsend between Third and Fourth

1871 San Francisco Glass Works, Newman & Duval proprietors, S Side King near Fourth, office 313 Davis

1872-1874 San Francisco Glass Works, Newman & Duval proprietors, S side King, near Fourth, office 313 Montgomery

1875-1876 San Francisco Glass Works, Carlton Newman proprietor, S Side King, near Fourth St., office 530 Washington

1876 The San Francisco and Pacific Glass Works merged, with the new company known as the San Francisco and Pacific Glass Works, with Carlton Newman as the proprietor.

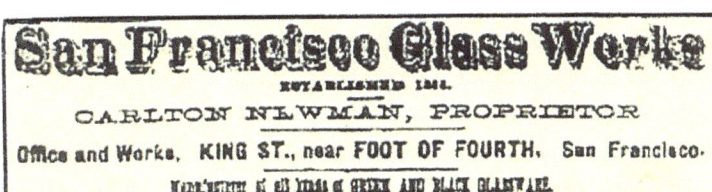

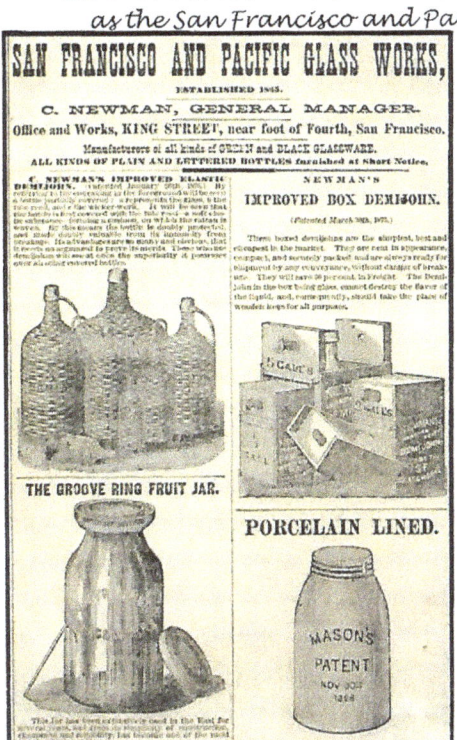

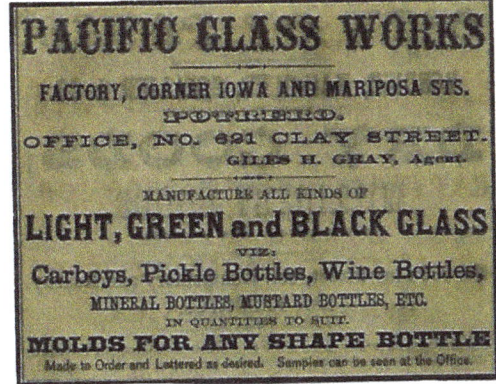

Front: SAN JOSE / SODA WORS / CAL.

Round, Smooth Base
Applied Top
Blue, $400.00 - 2021
Greenish Aqua, $300.00 - 2006
Aqua, $400.00 - 2021
Scarce
Circa: Late 1870's - 1886
Locale: San Jose, Cal
Note: "WORKS" is misspelled. Many have been dug in different towns around the bay, including Alameda, Benicia, Napa and Pacheco.

HISTORY: George Stenger is listed as the proprietor of thje San Jose Soda works from about 1878 until 1886. It was located at 350 Park Ave. After leaving the soda water business he became a bartender for George Schmidt who owned the Centennial Saloon in San Jose. The San Jose Soda Works was owned by John Balzhouse in later years, who preferred a Hutchinson type bottle.

Front: SAN LUIS OBISPO / SODA WATER / WORKS / S. CERIBELLI

Round, Smooth Base
Applied Top
Aqua, $300.00 - 2009, $600.00 - 2019
Rare
Variant: Gravitator Type
Circa: 1874-1882
Locale: San Luis Obispo, Cal.
Note: These bottles have been found in Cambria, Suisun City, and even in San Diego, as well as locally.

HISTORY: S. Ceribelli was listed as the proprietor of the San Luis Obispo soda works from 1874 to 1882. He must have used the gravitator bottle his last few years of ownership, as in 1883 a Mr. L. Martin was as proprietor of the soda works which had moved from Monterey St. to Higuera St.

Front: NATURAL MINERAL WATER / C. SCHNEER & CO. / SACRAMENTO / SOLE BOTTLERS

Round, Smooth Base
Tooled Top
Aqua
Rare
Varient: Hutch and Crown Top
Circa: 1892-1906
Locale: Sacramento, Cal.

HISTORY: Constant Schneer and Henry Postel were proprietors of the Capitol Soda Works prior to 1892. They were agents and bottlers of Fredericksburg Beer. Then from 1892 thru 1906 C. Schneer & Co. (Constant, Edward and Antoine Schneer) were listed as the proprietors of the Capitol Soda Works. Henry Postel must of sold his half of the company. They were located at 1111-1113 Front St from 1892 until 1889, and then at 310 K St. from 1899 thru 1906.

Front: C.A. SCHEIDEMANTEL / DENVER / COL.

Round, Smooth Base
Applied Top
Aqua
Varient: Denver, Colo in one line
$500.00 - 2007
Ex. Rare
Circa: 1875-1886
Locale: Denver, Colo.
Note: Ad circa 1878

C. A. SCHEIDEMANTEL,
SODA & SELTZER WATER
Manufacturer and Wholesale Dealer.
City and Country trade solicited.
609 Holladay Street,   DENVER, COLORADO.

HISTORY: 1876-1879 Scheidemantel, Charles A., 609 Holladay St.
         1880-1886 Scheidemantel, Charles A., 611 Holladay St.

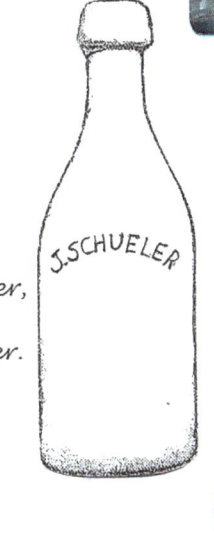

Front: J. SCHUELER

Round, Smooth Base
Applied Top
Aqua
Rare
Circa: 1866-1886
Locale: Denver, Colo.

HISTORY: 1866-1875, Jacob Schueler, soda manufacturer and bottler,
             376 Larimer
         1875-1886, Jacob Schueler, soda manufacturer and bottler.
             241 11th St.
         Ad circa 1866

Front: J. SCHUELER / DENVER, COL.
Re: A. & D.H.C.
Base: JS monogram

Round, Smooth Base
Applied Top
Aqua
Lt. Blue
Varient: Hutch
Rare
Circa: 1866-1886
Locale: Denver, Colo.

J. SCHUELER,
Formerly of A. Schinner & Co.,
CONFECTIONER
Larimer St., opposite the Post Office, Denver Colorado.
Manufacturer and Dealer in all kinds of
Confections, Candies, Cakes, Bread, Pies, Crackers
Fruits, Jellies, Nuts, Wines and Cigars, Soda Water, Ice Cream, and Fresh Oysters in
THEIR SEASON

HISTORY: See above bottle

Front: H.W. STOLL / LOS ANGELOS / SODA WORKS

Round Soda, Smooth Base
Applied Top
Aqua
Ex. Rare
Circa: Early 1870's
Locale: Los Angeles, Cal.
History: See page 48

Front: SHAIN & SIMMONS / DENVER

    Round, Smooth Base
    Tooled Top
    Aqua
    Varient: Hutch
    Ex. Rare
    Circa: 1892-1893
    Locale: Denver, Colo.

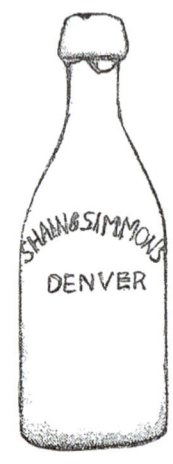

HISTORY: 1892-1893, Charles B. Shain and Frank C. Simmons, Bottling Works, 2163 Larimer

---

Front: J. SOMPS & J. MEILLETTE / AGENTS / COR OAK AND / BUENA VISTA AVE. / ALAMEDA
Re: NATURAL / MINERAL WATER / FROM THE / GOLDEN WEST / SPRINGS / NAPA / COUNTY CAL.

    Round, Smooth Base
    Tooled Top
    Aqua
    Rare
    Circa: 1892-1895
    Locale: Alameda, Cal.

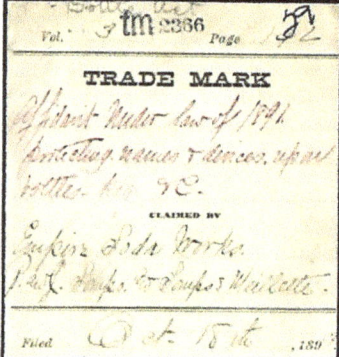

HISTORY: from 1892 to 1895 Jules S. Somps and Jean Meillette were listed as the proprietors of the Empire Soda Works in Alameda. They were located at 2301 Buena Vista Ave., corner of Oak. In 1895 Meillette sold his half of the business to another Somps, brother Peter Somps. Somps and Meillette trade marked the label shown above in 1893.

Front: P. SOMPS / MINERAL WATER / NAPA COUNTY / CAL.

    Round, Smooth Base
    Tooled Top
    Aqua
    Rare
    Circa: 1901-1906
    Locale: San Francisco

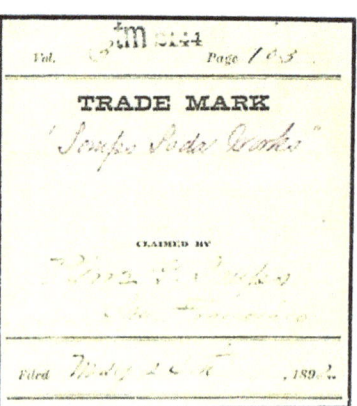

HISTORY: Peter Somps bought out the Golden West Soda Works from Pierre Somps and Frank Paillet sometime around 1900.
1901-1906, Somps, Peter, manufacturer of soda water, 624 Laguna, Tel Fell-423
Peter Somps applied for a trade mark for a label for Somps Soda Works, in 1892. This must have been for an earlier business venture. See at right.

Front: SHAIN & SIMMONS / DENVER

> Round, Smooth Base
> Tooled Top
> Aqua
> Varient: Hutch
> Ex. Rare
> Circa: 1892-1893
> Locale: Denver, Colo.

HISTORY: 1892-1893, Charles B. Shain and Frank C. Simmons, Bottling Works, 2163 Larimer

Front: J. SOMPS & J. MEILLETTE / AGENTS / COR OAK AND / BUENA VISTA AVE. / ALAMEDA
Re: NATURAL / MINERAL WATER / FROM THE / GOLDEN WEST / SPRINGS / NAPA / COUNTY CAL.

> Round, Smooth Base
> Tooled Top
> Aqua
> Rare
> Circa: 1892-1895
> Locale: Alameda, Cal.

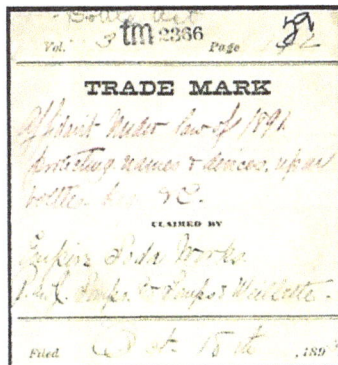

HISTORY: from 1892 to 1895 Jules S. Somps and Jean Meillette were listed as the proprietors of the Empire Soda Works in Alameda. They were located at 2301 Buena Vista Ave., corner of Oak. In 1895 Meillette sold his half of the business to another Somps, brother Peter Somps. Somps and Meillette trade marked the label shown above in 1893.

Front: P. SOMPS / MINERAL WATER / NAPA COUNTY / CAL.

> Round, Smooth Base
> Tooled Top
> Aqua
> Rare
> Circa: 1901-1906
> Locale: San Francisco

HISTORY: Peter Somps bought out the Golden West Soda Works from Pierre Somps and Frank Paillet sometime around 1900.
1901-1906, Somps, Peter, manufacturer of soda water, 624 Laguna, Tel Fell-423
Peter Somps applied for a trade mark for a label for Somps Soda Works, in 1892. This must have been for an earlier business venture. See at right.

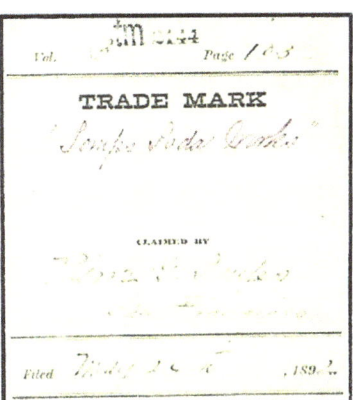

Front: TAYLOR & CO / VALPARAISO / CHILI
Re: SODA / WATER

Round, Iron Pontil
Applied Top
Green, $230.00 - 2010
Teal Green, $500.00 - 2017
Cobalt, $4400.00 - 2017
Teal Blue, $1800.00 - 2021
Scarce in Greens
Ex. Rare in Cobalt
Circa: 1850's
Locale: San Francisco or Sacramento
Note: These bottles have been found in Benicia, Sacramento and in San Francisco redevelopment areas. I have heard of one being found in the California coastal town of Trinidad, but cannot confirm this. Many of these bottles have been dug in North San Juan and Grass Valley.

HISTORY: This bottle is somewhat of a mystery. Most of this is conjecture. Asher S. Taylor must have arrived by ship in S.F. The ships often stop in Valparaiso to take on supplies and passengers. Records show Taylor made frequent trips there in 1850 and 1852. He must have had a source of water there and had bottles blown in the east, shipped to Valaparaiso to be filled and then shipped to S.F. or Sacramento for distribution. Asher Taylor was listed as the proprietor of the Jessie St. Soda Water Factory in 1854. This was not a street before 1854. In 1857 he was working at the Boley Soda Works in Sacramento. From 1858 to 1860 he is not listed anywhere. From 1861 to 1862 he is back in Sacramento in the soda water business. In 1862 he is has gone back to S.F. and was working at 222 Front, which was the address for the Connolly Bros. Geyser Soda Water Co. He again returned to Sacramento where between 1863 and 1869 he is listed as a resident. In 1870 Taylor is listed as a bitters manufacturer in Sac., with an address of O and 11th. And then back to S.F. as the agent and manufacturer of "Sparkling Medicated Bitters" at 1806 Powell St. Then in 1876, no doubt broke and out of ideas he became a drayman. Who really knows. Maybe the bottles were supposed to be distributed in Chili, and were shipped north by mistake. Or he thought it would make a good sales pitch, with soda from a exotic foreign country. The bottle is embossed as such after all.

Front: TAYLOR & Co. / SODA WATER / SAN FRANCISCO / EUREKA

Round, Iron Pontil
Applied Top
Cobalt, $1200.00 - 2021
Rare
Circa: 1851-1852
Locale: San Francisco
Note: This rare bottle has been dug in Georgetown, Cal., in the Gold Country.

HISTORY: The first advertisement was placed on April 2nd, 1852 in a San Francisco newspaper "Notice-the copartnership heretofore existing under the firm of Taylor & Co. Soda Manufacturers, is this day dissolved by mutual consent. The business will here after be conducted by Wm. H. Taylor. W.H. Taylor, James P. Bradish, Charles J. Stokes"
On July 27th, 1852, Wm. H. Taylor disposed of his interest and business in the Mineral Water Manufacturer.
No mention of Asher Taylor involved with this company.

TAYLOR, ASHER S.

This bottle is from Taylor's New York City business from 1847 to 1848. He came around the horn to set up a Western soda business in 1849 and must have brought some of his Eastern bottles and soda water apparatus with him. Only two are known and both dug up about 2010 in the vicinity of the Monterey Customs House. Taylor went on to begin the Taylor & Co. Valparaiso Chili soda company although nobody is sure if his office was San Francisco or Sacramento. San Francisco seems like the logical choice.

Mike Southworth Collection

Front: TOLENAS / SODA / SPRINGS
Re: NATURAL / MINERAL WATER

Round, Smooth Base
Applied and Tooled Top
Aqua
Lime Green
Lt. Green, $210.00 - 2018
Common in Aqua
Rare in Green
Varient: Crown Top
    Base has T.BROS.
    Re. has TOLENAS / SODA / SPRINGS
Circa: 1885-1906
Locale: San Francisco

HISTORY: This spring was located about 4 miles north of Fairfield in Solano County.
  1885-1886, John C. Remington, agent for Tolenas Springs Soda Water, 217 Commercial St.
  1887-1900, Charles Eggars and Sidney S. Gould, agents for Tolenas Soda Water, 1308 Mission
  1900-1906 Tolenas Mineral Water Co., 1123 Howard St.
  In the early 1900's the Tolenas Soda Water Co. also has an agency in Sacramento, at 821 K St. This may account for the bottles with 'T. Bros.' on the base.

Front: UNION / SODA WORKS

Round, Smooth Base
Applied Top
Aqua, $450.00 - 2018
Varient: Hutch
Ex. Rare
Circa: Late 1870's to Early 1880's
Locale: Tombstone, Arizona
Note: This rare bottle is generally found in early Arizona mining camps. The author personally picked up pieces of at least 15 broken examples at a mine site on the outskirts of Tombstone.

HISTORY: Blush & Buddington were listed as the proprietors of the Union Soda Works. It was located on the corner of 2nd St. and Charleston Rd. Due to the lack of early directories we do not know how long they were in business. This is the only blob top soda from Arizona and is a territorial bottle. It was blown in San Francisco, and has the western curved R's.

Front: UKIAH SODA WORKS / UKIAH, CAL.

Round, Smooth Base
Applied Top
Cobalt
Ex. Rare, possibly unique
Variant: Hutch
Circa: 1870's (approx.)
Locale: Ukiah, Cal.
Note: From the Gary Engle collection and dug at the dump site of the Ukiah Soda Works.

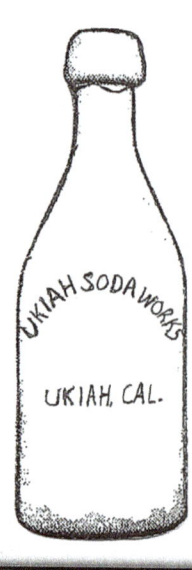

HISTORY: There is a hutch style bottle from Ukiah that dates from 1883 to about 1890. G.W. Eppler was listed as proprietor of the soda works at this time. The blob top bottle predates this and may have no connection to Eppler. No other info.

Front: UNION SODA WORKS / 'ACID BOTTLE' / SAN FRANCISCO
Re: THOMPSON'S / PREMIUM / MINERAL WATER

Round Ten Pin, Smooth Base
Applied Top
Aqua, $500.00 - 2021
Greenish Aqua, $220.00 - 2019
Rare
Variant: without the word "PREMIUM"
Circa: 1872-1895
Locale: San Francisco
Note: Ad below circa 1877.

HISTORY: George C. Thompson established his soda and mineral water business in 1850, address unknown. He worked in this type of business for 55 years until 1905. He applied for a trade mark for Acid Water in 1872. See drawing above. In 1895 started to devote all his time and efforts in selling fountain soda water and supplies, and ceased the bottling of mineral and soda water. Thompson was only bottling 50 dozen bottles pre day at his height of business, which is one reason these bottles are rare. The competition was bottling as much as 200 or 300 dozen per day. His 50 dozen a day was not much, considering the demand for soda and mineral water at this time.

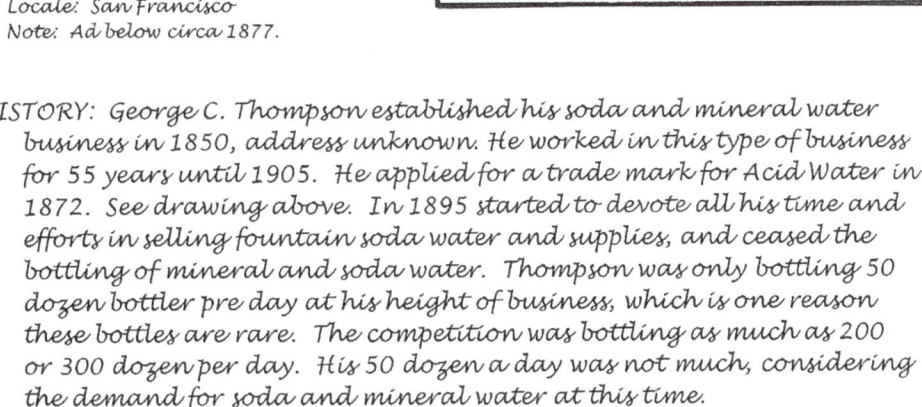

Front: J.R. VANCE / COL.
Re: I.G.CO.

Round, Smooth Base
Applied Top
Aqua, $200.00 - 2021
Rare
Circa: 1881-1886
Locale: Salida, Alpine and Poncha Springs, Colo.

HISTORY: J.R. Vance was listed as a bottler in Alpine in 1881, Poncha Springs in 1882, and in Salida, 1883-1886. This bottle was probably used in all 3 locations.

Front: VICHY SPRINGS / NAPA CO / CAL
Re: NATURAL / MINERAL WATER
Base: S.F.

Round, Smooth Base
Tooled Top
Aqua
Common
Varient: Crown Top, Base is plain
Circa: 1898-1906
Locale: San Francisco
Note: Label trade marked in 1899 by
G. Lepori, S.F. See at right.

HISTORY: 1898-1907 "YOUNG'S" added to the back of bottle. The rest of the embossing is the same. See Young's Natural Mineral Water.
    1898-1901 Lepori's Napa Vichy Mineral water, Bertin & Lepori agents, 520-522 Washington
    1902-1906 Bertin & Lepori, wholesale groceries and proprietor of the Eagle Cigar Co., Eagle Coffee and Spice Mills, and agents for Lepori's Napa Vichy Mineral Water, 520-522 Washington.

Front: VERNON MINERAL / WATER

Round, Smooth Base
Applied Top
Aqua
Ex. Rare, possibly unique
Circa: 1874-1878
Locale: San Francisco
Note: From the collection of Eric McGuire.

HISTORY: 1874 Isaac A. Kenny, Agent Vernon Mineral Water, 237 Montgomery
    1875-1878 William H. Bovee, Nestel Bovee, agents for Vernon Mineral Water, 238 Montgomery
    After 1878 there was further listing of Vernon Mineral Water in S.F. The spring was located in Oakland, a farmer by the name of Josiah Sessions bottled this water and sold it in San Francisco.

Front: WALTER'S / NAPA / TRADE / "HORSESHOE" / MARK / COUNTY / SODA
Re: MINERAL WATER / FROM / WALTER'S / SODA / SPRINGS
Base: HERVE & SOMPS AGTS

Round, Smooth Base
Applied and Tooled Top
Aqua
Rare
Circa: 1890-1891
Locale: San Francisco

HISTORY: 1890-1891 Herve & Co. (E.F. Herve and Pierre G. Somps), agents mineral waters, sw cor O'Farrell and Mason

Front: WALTER'S / NAPA / TRADE / 'HORSESHOE' / MARK / COUNTY / SODA
Re: MINERAL WATER / FROM / WALTER'S / SODA / SPRINGS

Round, Smooth Base
Applied and Tooled Top
Aqua, A.T., $50.00 - 2021
Common
Varient: Hutch
Circa: 1886-1899
Locale: San Francisco
Note: Bottle was trade marked in 1893 by J.J. Walters & J.W. Smittle
See drawing at right.

HISTORY: Walter's Springs was discovered by Gustave Walter in 1885. They located in Pope Valley, east of St. Helena, near present day Lake Berryessa.

1886-1887 Walter's Napa County Soda Co., F.G. Walter & F. Franz, 114 Stockton
1887-1888 Walter, Gustave & Co. (John H. Roberts), proprietor Wigwam and Orpheum Theater and Walter's Soda Springs, Napa Co., office 114 Stockton
1889-1890 Walter, Gustave and Co., managers and proprietors Orpheum Theater, 113-119 O'Farrell, the Rathskelter Junction Market, Turk & Mason
1889-1890 Herve, Adolph J., agent Walter's Napa County Soda, office Orpheum Bldg.
1890-1891 Herve & Co. (Pierre Somps), agents mineral waters, sw cor O'Farrell and Mason
1892-1894 Walter's Napa Soda, the leading mineral water, depot 641 Mission, G.L. Abell Sole Agent
1895-1898 Phillips, Samuel, lessee and manager Walter's Napa County Soda, 404 McAllister
1899   Phillips's Napa County Soda Co. Inc. (formerly Walters Napa County Soda, S.A. Phillips manager, 717 McAllister, Tel Mint 1481

Front: WATSONVILLE / CIDER & GINGER ALE CO. / INC. / S.F. CAL.

Round, Smooth Base
Applied and Tooled Top
Aqua
Rare
Circa: 1880's - 1890's (approx..)
Locale: San Francisco

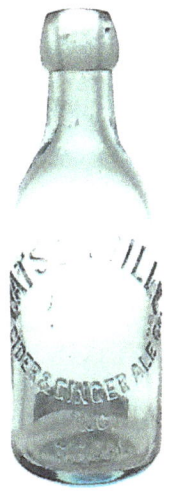

HISTORY: No info at this time. Appears to a competitor of Martinelli of Watsonville.

Front: W & B / SHASTA
Re: UNION GLASS WORKS PHILAD / SUPERIOR / MINERAL WATER

Round, 10 Sided Mug Base, Iron Pontil
Applied Top
Cobalt, $14,000.00 - 2010
Ex. Rare
Circa: 1853-1858 (approx)
Locale: Shasta, Cal.
Note: The few examples of this rare bottle that exist were found in Old Shasta. There have also been a few broken specimens found in the Red Bluff, Cal. area.

HISTORY: The first listing for S.B. Westcott and B.L. Bartlett was in 1853. They were located at 13 Front St. Sacramento as soda water manufacturers. We believe they were using this address as an office for their soda water factory and store in Shasta. The reason for this belief, there were also at this address, the companies of John Molitor, Henry and William Sheridan, A.C. Hamilton and Julius Hollister, listed as soda water manufacturers. In 1857 W & B had for sale 1/3 or ½ interest in their soda factory and other property in Shasta. Reference was to be made at Cudworth & Co., San Francisco, which means that A.W. Cudworth may been a partner in this company also.

Front: W & D / SALT LAKE CITY / UTAH

Round, Smooth Base
Applied Top
Aqua
Ex. Rare
Circa: late 1870's
Locale: Salt Lake City, Utah

HISTORY: It is believed that this bottle was used by Whiting and Denhalter to bottle soda water in the 1870's. A territorial bottle.

Front: Wm WILSON / BUTTE CITY / M.T.

Round, Smooth Base
Applied Top
Aqua
Ex. Rare
Circa: 1880's
Locale: Butte City, Montana
Note: One of the rarest bottles from Montana.

HISTORY: No info at this time. A territorial bottle.

Front: WILLIAMS / & / SEVERANCE

    Round, Iron and Open Pontil
Applied Top
Teal Green I.P., $700.00 - 2017
Blue, I.P., $1200.00 - 2021
Blue, O.P., $160.00 - 2017 (repaired)
Rare with Iron pontil
Ex. Rare with Open Pontil
Ex. Rare in Green
Circa: 1852-1853
Locale: San Francisco

HISTORY: Lewellyn Williams and Henry Severance arrived in San Francisco sometime between Sept. and Nov. 1851. The partnership dissolved on Oct. 13th 1853.

1852 Williams & Severance, Soda manufacturers, Vallejo above Dupont
      Williams, Lewis, Soda manufacturer, Vallejo between Stockton and Dupont
      Severance, Henry, Mineral Water, Vallejo between Stockton and Dupont
      Williams, Lewellyn, Soda manufacturer, 246 Powell

1853 Williams & Severance, Soda Water Factory, Vallejo between Dupont and Stockton
      Williams, Lewellyn, Soda Water Factory, Vallejo between Dupont and Stockton
      Severance, Luther, at Williams & Severance Soda Factory

---

Front: WILLIAMS / & SEVERANCE / SAN FRANCISCO / CAL.
Re: SODA & / MINERAL WATER

    Round, Iron Pontil
Applied Top
Green, $1700.00 - 2017
        $1200.00 - 2021
Cobalt, $1300.00 - 2021
Rare
Ex. Rare with Double Collar Top
Varient: Double Collar Top
Circa: 1852-1853
Locale: San Francisco
Note: Ad from the 1854 San Francisco Directory. This ad ran despite the partnership dissolving in Oct. 1853.
Many of these bottles were found in a filled in creek bed in the Benicia Arsenal in 1987. At least 20, all were broken, including one that was very light green, almost aqua. This creek had 100's of broken 1850's era bottles, but these were the only sodas.

HISTORY: See previous bottle.

WILLIAMS & SEVERANCE,
MANUFACTURERS OF
SODA AND MINERAL WATERS
VALLEJO STREET,
(Between Dupont and Stockton)
SAN FRANCISCO, CALIFORNIA.

Front: HENRY, WINKLE / SAC. CITY
Re: X X

Round, Iron and Open Pontil
Applied Top
Aqua, $425.00 - 2021
Scarce with Iron Pontil
Ex. Rare with Open Pontil
Circa: 1852-1854
Locale: Sacramento, Cal.

HISTORY: According to the research done, Henry Winkle may have never actually been in the soda water manufacturing business. He arrived in Sacramento sometime in 1850 and opened a coffee restaurant and bakery. He also did some work in the real estate business. On Nov. 2, 1852, the city was destroyed by fire, and Winkle lost everything. He then rebuilt, and one month later, Dec. 1852 and Jan. 1853, the city was flooded. Winkle was financially ruined with property values decreased to 15 cents on the dollar. He moved to S.F. in 1854. He then opened a bakery on Vallejo and Battery Sts., where he did a large business until 1871. Later he went into the wine and liquor trade, see ad from 1876 above. He was also connected to the first cement made on the Pacific Coast.

We believe that the bottle listed above was actually used by Alleman & Stratton, who were Soda Water manufacturers in Sacramento, as well as the gold rush towns of Fiddletown, and Michigan Bar, from 1852 to 1855. Winkle was never listed as a soda water manufacturer, Alleman and Stratton were, established in 1852 with a capacity of 500 dozen bottles a day. With them filling so many bottles you would think at least one would have turned up by now. Instead we find Winkle's bottles all over the Gold Country and Sacramento. The big fire of 1852 did not touch Alleman & Stratton's soda water factory as it was located in the Alley, between M and N, and Second and Third Sts. They must have acquired Winkle's bottles after the fire.

Front: AUG. WINKLER / S.B. / SODA WORKS

Round, Smooth Base
Applied Top
Aqua
Rare
Varient: Hutch
Circa: 1876-1886 (approx)
Locale: San Bernardino, Cal.

HISTORY: From 1876 to 1883 August Winkler was listed as being a liquor and soda factory proprietor on Third St, in San Bernardino. In 1883 he was listed as the proprietor of Winkler's Soda Works now off 3rd between C & D, where he lasted until 1887 when he passed away. His widow then sold the soda works to C.F. Riley.

Front: WOOD'S / NAPA / SODA
Re: NATURAL / MINERAL WATER

Round, Smooth Base
Applied Top
Aqua, $275.00 - 2009
Teal Blue, $500.00 - 2021
Green, Cobalt
Rare
Circa: 1868-1873
Locale: San Francisco
Note: A couple of these were dug in the Benicia Arsenal in 1976, and they have also been dug in Grass Valley.

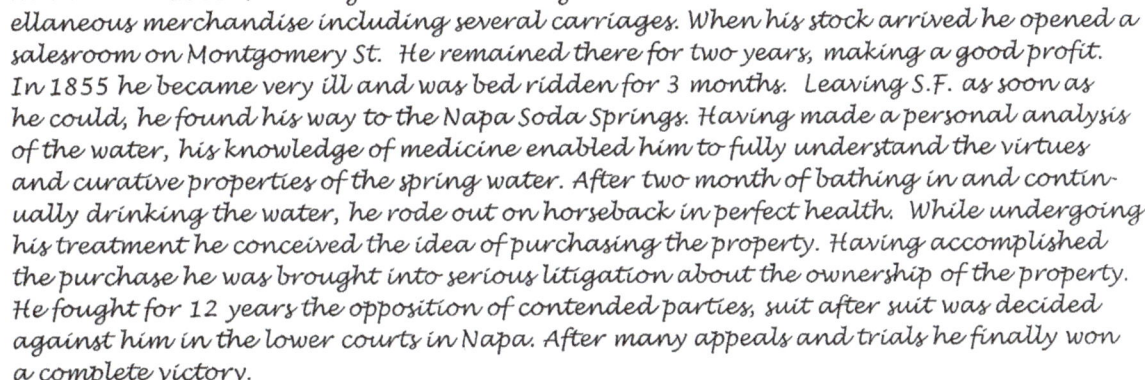

HISTORY: J. Henry Wood was born in New York state in 1818. He was a partner a retail dry goods firm. With his health failing he decided to retire from active business affairs. He concluded he would try the health giving climate of California and left New York in 1853. He brought with him large number is miscellaneous merchandise including several carriages. When his stock arrived he opened a salesroom on Montgomery St. He remained there for two years, making a good profit. In 1855 he became very ill and was bed ridden for 3 months. Leaving S.F. as soon as he could, he found his way to the Napa Soda Springs. Having made a personal analysis of the water, his knowledge of medicine enabled him to fully understand the virtues and curative properties of the spring water. After two month of bathing in and continually drinking the water, he rode out on horseback in perfect health. While undergoing his treatment he conceived the idea of purchasing the property. Having accomplished the purchase he was brought into serious litigation about the ownership of the property. He fought for 12 years the opposition of contended parties, suit after suit was decided against him in the lower courts in Napa. After many appeals and trials he finally won a complete victory.

The property was worth a large amount and in the year 1861, the receiver, who was court appointed, paid Dr. Wood a profit of $12,000.00. The annual income of the springs would increase when, in 1862 Dr. Wood decided to bottle and sell the water for public use. He made many improvements to the springs and surrounding land. He planted a vineyard in 1862, he made the first Hock Wine on the Pacific Coast. He retired from business life in 1872. Dr. Wood trade marked his bottle in 1871, see drawing.. The Napa Soda Springs ad is circa 1870's.

1868-1869 Wood, J. Henry, Proprietor Napa Soda Springs, Office #1 Masonic Temple
1870-1873 Napa Wood Company, depot 122 Berry, Office 418 Montgomery

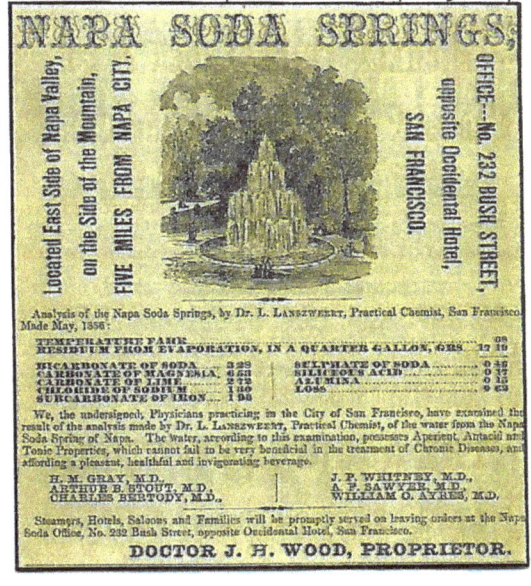

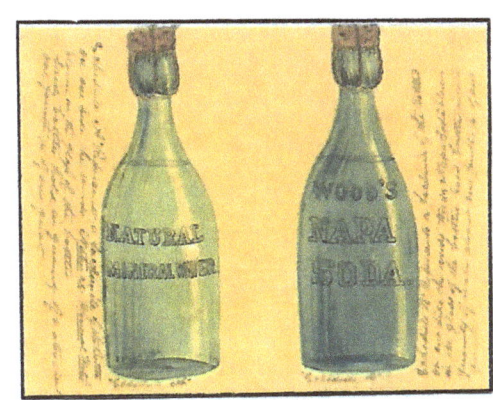

Front: WM & D / SALT LAKE CITY / UTAH
Re: A. & D.H.C.

    Round, Smooth Base
    Applied Top
    Aqua
    Ex. Rare
    Circa: Late 1870's - Early 1880's
    Locale: Salt Lake City, Utah

HISTORY: *No info at this time. A territorial bottle.*

Front: HENRY G. WURTZ / GRAND JUNCTION / COLORADO

    Round, Smooth Base
    Tooled Top
    Aqua
    Ex. Rare
    Varient: Hutch
    Circa: 1889-1893
    Locale: Grand Junction, Colo.

HISTORY: *1889-1893 Wurtz, Henry G., manufacturer and bottler of soda, no address given.*

Front: X.L.C.R. / SODA WORKS / SAN FRANCISCO

    Round, Smooth Base
    Applied Top
    Green
    Aqua, $1300.00 - 2009
    Ex. Rare
    Circa: 1861-1872
    Note: San Francisco and Benicia have yielded examples of this bottle.

HISTORY: 1861-1862   Brader (Louis) & Co. (Peter Brader), Excelsior Soda Works, 525 Vallejo
                1862-1863   Brader (Louis) & Co. (Peter & Henry Brader), Excelsior Soda Works, 738 Broadway
                1863-1864   Brader (Henry) & Co. (William Hartman), Excelsior Soda Works, 734 Broadway
                1865-1866   Brader, Henry, Excelsior Bottling Establishment, 611 Battery
                1867-1868   Brader, Henry, Excelsior Bottling Establishment, 738 Broadway
                1868-1869   Excelsior Soda Factory, Henry Brader proprietor, 738 Broadway
                1870-1871   Brader Bros. (Christian & Peter), Excelsior Soda Factory, 738 Broadway
                1871-1872   Brader Bros. (Henry & Louis), Excelsior Soda Works, 738 Broadway
                1872-1873   Excelsior Bottling Establishment, Henry Brader proprietor, 738 Broadway

Front: YOUNG'S / NATURAL / MINERAL / WATER
Re: VICHY SPRINGS / NAPA CO. / CAL.

    Round, Smooth Base
    Tooled Top
    Ex. Rare in Lime Green
    Aqua, $200.00 - 2021
    Circa: 1898-1901
    Locale: San Francisco

HISTORY: 1898-1901   *Young's Vichy Springs Mineral Water Company, L. Long president, 1200 Webster*

Front: W.S. WRIGHT
Base: PACIFIC GLASS WORKS

Round, Smooth Base
Applied Top
Green
Deep Aqua, $1100.00 - 2021
Greenish Aqua, $1500.00 - 2017
Teal, $1900.00 - 2021
Scarce in Aquas
Ex. Rare in Darker Colors
Circa: 1861-1867
Locale: Virginia City, Nevada

HISTORY: William S. Wright started up his soda works in 1861. It was the first soda manufactory in Nevada. He was also the first merchant of any kind to use embossed bottles with his name on them, in Nevada. In 1863 Wright ordered 24,000 bottles from the then new Pacific Glass Works. It was no doubt the first large order for the new glass house. It was big news at the time, and made the papers in San Francisco and Sacramento. Wright's Soda Factory was located at 124 North B St. at Mill. In mid 1867 Wright sold his business, perhaps to George Morrill, who started selling soda water in his drug store about this same time. This is the earliest embossed territory bottle in the U.S. There are only about two dozen mint bottles known with probably about the same amount slight damaged. It's a mystery of what happened to the rest of the order of 24,000. Surely many were lost in transit, but somewhere out there is a whole lot of W.S. Wright bottles waiting to be found. Ad below is circa 1862.

WILLIAM S. WRIGHT,
SODA MANUFACTURER,
CORNER MILL AND B STREETS,
VIRGINIA CITY.

☞ Soda delivered to all parts of the City and County, by wagon or Stages. Orders thankfully received and punctually attended to.

Front: ZAREMBO

Round Torpedo Shape, Smooth Base
Applied Top
Aqua
Rare
Circa: 1880's-1890's
Locale: Seattle, Wash.

HISTORY: No info at this time.

GRAVITATOR TYPES

Front: AMADOR COUNTY / SODA WORKS

Round, Smooth Base
Applied Top
Aqua
Rare
Varient: Crown Top
Circa: 1879-1891
Locale: Jackson, Cal.

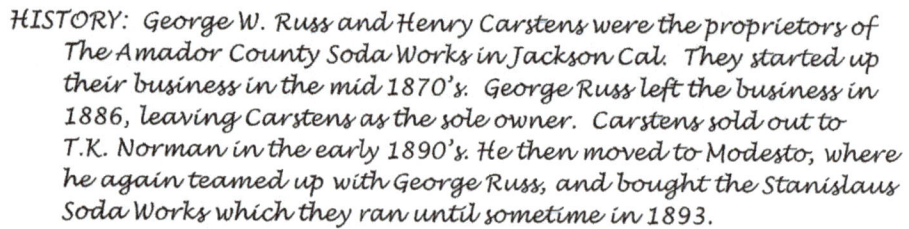

HISTORY: George W. Russ and Henry Carstens were the proprietors of The Amador County Soda Works in Jackson Cal. They started up their business in the mid 1870's. George Russ left the business in 1886, leaving Carstens as the sole owner. Carstens sold out to T.K. Norman in the early 1890's. He then moved to Modesto, where he again teamed up with George Russ, and bought the Stanislaus Soda Works which they ran until sometime in 1893.

Front: B (block letter)

Round, Smooth Base
Applied and Tooled Top
Aqua
Common
Varient: Blob and Crown Top
Circa: 1870-1910
Locale: Stockton and Marysville. Cal.

HISTORY: Charles Belding was in business with Benjamin Lippincott for many years. In 1870 Belding bought out the interest of Lippincott. The soda factory in Marysville was known as Belding Soda Works by 1894, run by Charles Belding's brother Lyman. In 1895 Belding sold part interest in the Stockton location to Samuel B. Huskins. The company was known as Belding and Huskins Soda Works until 1910 when it closed down. The bottle listed above should date from the early 1880's to around 1900 when the crown top became popular. See "B" in the blob top section.

Front: B / STOCKTON

Round, Smooth Base
Applied Top
Aqua
Scarce
Circa: 1880's-1900
Locale: Stockton, Cal.

HISTORY: See above bottle and 'B' in the blob top section.

Front: BAY CITY SODA WATER Co. / SAN FRANCISCO / CAL.

Round, Smooth Base
Applied and Tooled Top
Aqua
Scarce
Variant: Blob Top
*   without the word "CAL"*
Circa: 1871-1913
Locale: San Francisco

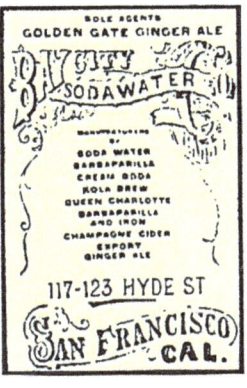

HISTORY: See "BAY CITY" in the blob top section. The bottle listed above was probably used from the mid 1880's until the soda works closed its doors in 1913.

Front: E.L. BILLINGS / SACRAMENTO / CAL.

Round, Smooth Base
Applied Top
Aqua
Common
Varient: Crown Top and Codd Type
Circa: 1866-1883
Locale: Sacramento, Cal.

HISTORY: See "E.L. BILLINGS" in the blob top section. The bottle listed above should date from the mid 1870's until 1883.

Front: J.I. BLIVENS & Co. / OAKLAND / CAL.

Round, Smooth Base
Applied Top
Aqua
Lime Green
Scarce in Aqua
Ex. Rare in Greens
Circa: 1872-1880
Locale: Oakland, Cal.

History: James Blevins started the Pioneer Soda works in Oakland in 1872. It was located at 665 Broadway. He was also an agent for Pacific Congress Water at this location. In 1875 Blivens moved to 13th and Franklin Sts.. Then in 1877 he took a John D. Taylor as a part owner. In 1880 Blivens went to San Francisco and Paul Lohse joined John Taylor as the new proprietors on the Pioneer Soda Works, still located at 13th and Franklin Sts.

Front: BOWLAND & CRAIG / CITY PHARMACY / SODA WORKS / SAN BERNARDINE

Round, Smooth Base
Applied Top
Aqua
Ex. Rare
Circa: 1874-1876
Locale: San Bernardino, Cal.
Note: "San Bernardino" is misspelled

HISTORY: Felding Bowland and Dr. William Craig were the proprietors of the City Pharmacy from 1873 to 1876. They were located opposite the Post Office in San Bernardino. In 1874 they acquired a soda water machine and started to manufacture soda water. In 1876 Dr. Craig returned to Riverside to manage his hotel, which he established in 1871, thus the end of the partnership. But then in 1879, Bowland was again listed in the soda water business as the proprietor of the Crystal Soda Water Factory in San Bernardino.

Front: CASEY & CRONAN / EAGLE / SODA WORKS

Round, Smooth Base
Applied Top
Aqua
Lime Green
Common in Aqua
Ex. Rare in Greens
Circa: 1875-1886
Locale: Sacramento, Cal.
Note: One of the few gravitators that come in any color other than aqua.

HISTORY: The partnership of Hugh Casey and Michael Cronan was formed in 1875, when former partner Hugh Kelly passed away. They were located at 50 K St. in Sacramento until 1886, when M. Cronan left to form his own business. Hugh Casey continued as the proprietor of the Eagle Soda Works until 1905.

Front: CIRCLE POULSON & CO. / RED BLUFF / CALA.

Round, Smooth Base
Applied Top
Aqua
Rare
Circa: 1880-1885 (approx)
Locale: Red Bluff, Cal.

HISTORY: It is believed that Circle Poulson & Co. bottled soda water in Red Bluff for a very short time in the 1880's, and possibly the late 1870's. Info is very scarce on the bottle.

Front: W.E. DEAMER
Re: GRASS VALLEY / CAL.

Round, Smooth Base
Applied and Tooled Top
Aqua
Scarce
Varient: Blob Top
Circa: 1870-1890
Locale: Grass Valley, Cal.

HISTORY: W.E. Deamer's soda works was listed at the corner of School and Richardson Sts. in the 1870's and 1880's. He was listed as being a manufacturer of ale, soda water and cider. See "DEAMER" in the blob top section. The bottles listed here should around 1880 to 1890. Prior to the 1880's Deamer most likely used the blob top bottle.

Front: W.E. DEAMER
Re: NEVADA / SODA WATER CO. / GRASS VALLEY / NEVADA CO. / CAL.

Round, Smooth Base
Applied Top
Aqua
Lt. Green
Scarce
Varient: Blob Top
Circa: 1870-1890
Locale: Grass Valley, Cal.
Note: Many cases of this and other soda bottles were found in the basement of a building in Grass Valley in the 1970's.

HISTORY: See above bottle.

Front: EMPIRE SODA WORKS / VALLEJO

Round, Smooth Base
Applied Top
Aqua
Scarce
Varient: Blob and Crown Top
Circa: 1874-1890
Locale: Vallejo, Cal.
Note: Usually found in the neighboring towns around Vallejo such as Crockett, Napa, Benicia, Martinez, Pacheco and Port Costa. Most of the bottles used in Vallejo must have been returned to the Soda Works.

HISTORY: See "EMPIRE SODA WORKS" in the blob top section. The bottle listed here should date from around 1880 to 1890.

Front: HOLLISTER & CO. / HONOLULU

> Round, Smooth Base
> Applied Top
> Aqua
> Ex. Rare
> Circa: 1870's - 1880's

History: See blob top section.

Front: LEVY BROS. / PORTLAND / OREGON
Re: LB (monogram)

> Round, Smooth Base
> Applied Top
> Aqua, $650.00 - 2019
> Ex. Rare
> Circa: 1870's-1880's
> Locale: Portland, Oregon
> Note: One of these rare bottles was dug by the author in West Berkeley, Cal. in 2012. Somebody traveling on a ship, or on a train, probably brought it down than discarded it in a privy.

HISTORY: No info available at this time.

Front: E. & J. LODTMANN / SANTA CRUZ CO. / CAL.

> Round, Smooth Base
> Applied and Tooled Top
> Aqua
> Scarce
> Varient: "J. LODTMANN" instead of "E. & J"
> Circa: 1875-1890 (approx.)
> Locale: Santa Cruz, Cal.

HISTORY: Ernest and Justus Lodtmann moved their soda water manufacturing business from Knights Ferry to Santa Cruz in 1875. They ran the soda works together until around 1885 when Ernest left and Justus ran the business alone until sometime in 1890. Hence the two varients of this bottle. In 1890 the Lodtmanns sold the Santa Cruz Soda Works to Peter Wesselhoeft.

Base: MARYSVILLE SODA WORKS

> Round, Smooth Base
> Tooled Top
> Aqua
> Rare
> Circa: 1880's - 1890's
> Locale: Marysville, Cal.

HISTORY: I believe this bottle was used by Belding and Lippincott in Marysville before Charles Belding took over sole ownership in 1894.

Front: A. MONROE & CO. / EUREKA H.B. / CAL.

Round, Smooth Base
Applied Top
Aqua
Scarce
Circa: Late 1870's to 1887
Locale: Eureka, Cal.

HISTORY: Alonzo Monroe started bottling soda water at the Humboldt Soda Works and Brewing Co. in 1876. It was located on the northeast corner of 5th and A Sts. Before Alonzo Monroe died in 1884, Monroe turned the company over to his sons, John W. Monroe and Joe. D. Monroe. They ran the company together until 1887. In 1887 John Monroe started his own soda works in Springville, leaving Joe to run the soda works in Eureka. Joe Monroe changed the name to J.P. Monroe Co. The two bottles listed here should date from about 1876 to the late 1880's.

Front: J.P. MONROE / EUREKA / HUMBOLDT CO. / CAL.

Round, Smooth Base
Applied Top
Lt. Green
Aqua
Scarce
Circa: 1887-1890
Locale: Eureka, Cal.

HISTORY: See above bottle.
Joseph P. Monroe was listed in the soda water business on the southeast corner of A and Washington Sts.

Front: NEVADA / SODA WATER CO. / GRASS VALLEY / NEVADA CO. / CAL.

Round, Smooth Base
Applied Top
Aqua
Scarce
Circa: 1880-1890
Locale: Grass Valley, Cal.

HISTORY: See W.E. Deamer in the blob top section and in this section.

Front: PACIFIC / & / PUGET SOUND SODA WORKS / SEATTLE / W.T.

    Round, Smooth Base
    Applied Top
    Aqua, $275.00 - 2011
    Rare
    Circa: Late 1870's - 1880's
    Locale: Seattle, Wash.

HISTORY: No info at this time. A territory bottle.

Front: PEARSON BROS. / BODIE

    Round, Smooth Base
    Applied Top
    Aqua, $3600.00 - 2009, $2800.00 - 2012
           $1500.00 - 2019
    Ex. Rare
    Circa: 1882-1891 (approx.)
    Locale: Bodie, Cal.

HISTORY: See Pearson Bros. in the blob top section.

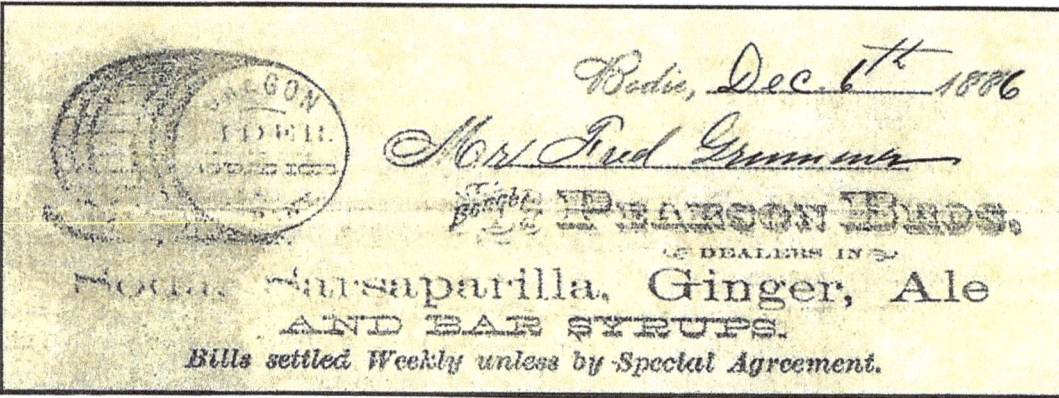

Front: S.L.O. / SODA WATER / S. CERIBELLI

    Round, Smooth Base
    Applied Top
    Lt. Green
    Aqua
    Scarce
    Varient: Blob and Crown Top
    Circa: 1874-1882
    Locale: San Luis Obispo, Cal.

HISTORY: S. Ceribelli was the proprietor of the San Luis Obispo Soda Works from 1874-1882. It was located on Montgomery St. The bottle listed here should date from the late 1870's to 1882.

Front: STEPHENS & JOSE / VIRGINIA CITY / NEVADA
Re: S J (monogram)

Round, Smooth Base
Applied Top
Aqua, $1800.00 - 2008
Ex. Rare
Circa: 1874 only
Locale: Virginia City, Nevada
Note: Usually found in the Carson City, Virginia City area, one was dug in Marin Co. Cal. in the early 2000's.

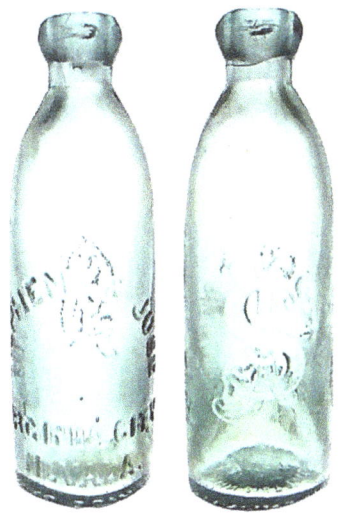

HISTORY: The Stephens and Jose soda works was located on C St., between Gold Hill and Virginia City. They did not last long and must have gone out of business before the fire of 1875, as it did not reach their place of business. After the partnership ended, Alfred Jose must have got the soda apparatus and delivery wagon as he went to Reno and opened the Reno Soda factory in late 1875. Ad is circa 1875.

> **RENO SODA FACTORY.**
> Virginia Street, Reno.
> **ALFRED JOSE,**
> MANUFACTURER OF
> Oregon Champagne Cider,
> Belfast Ginger Ale,
> Soda Water, Porter and Ale,
> and Syrups of all kinds.
> sep26 tf

Front: P. J. S. & CO. / SONOMA / CAL.

Round, Smooth Base
Applied Top
Aqua
Lime Green
Ex. Rare
Circa: 1875-1883
Locale: Santa Rosa, Cal.

HISTORY: Patrick J. Sullivan started the Santa Rosa Soda Works in 1875. It was located at 160 Third St. This is the first bottle used by Sullivan The second one had his name embossed fully on it.

Front: P.J. SULLIVAN / SANTA ROSA / CAL.

Round, Smooth Base
Applied Top
Aqua
Ex. Rare
Circa: 1875-1883
Locale: Santa Rosa, Cal.

HISTORY: See above bottle.

Front: T & H / SONOMA / CAL.

Round, Smooth Base
Applied Top
Aqua
Lime Green
Ex. Rare
Circa: 1876-1878
Locale: Santa Rosa, Cal.

HISTORY: John Thomas and a Mr. Haskins were the proprietors of the Sonoma Soda Works, located 112 Second St., corner of Wilson. This partnership only lasted about two years as Haskins left the company and Thomas became the sole proprietor. Bottles used after 1878 are embossed with just "T & Co. See below. In 1882 Thomas sold out to George Ford and Conrad Johnson.

Front: T & Co. / SONOMA / CAL.

Round, Smooth Base
Applied Top
Aqua
Teal Blue
Ex. Rare
Circa: 1878-1882
Locale: Santa Rosa, Cal.

HISTORY: See above bottle.

Front: TAYLOR & LOHSE / SUCCESSORS TO / J.I. BLIVENS & CO. / OAKLAND / CAL.

Round, Smooth Base
Applied Top
Aqua
Scarce
Circa: 1880-1889
Locale: Oakland, Cal.

HISTORY: James Blivens left the Pioneer Soda Works in 1880. At that point Paul Lohse joined John Taylor as the proprietors. They were also agents for Eastern Cider, Pacific Congress Springs and Seltzer Water and the Litton Springs Seltzer Water. In 1884 Taylor and Lohse moved the business to 13th and Webster Sts., where they remained until 1889 when Paul Lohse left the company.

Front: JOHN D. TAYLOR & CO. / PIONEER SODA WORKS / OAKLAND / CAL.

Round, Smooth Base
Applied Top
Aqua
Rare
Circa: 1880's
Locale: Oakland, Cal.

Front: WILLIAMS BROS. / SAN JOSE / CAL.

Round, Smooth Base
Applied Top
Lt. Green
Aqua
Common
Varient: Hutch and Crown Top
Circa: 1871-1910
Locale: San Jose, Cal.

HISTORY: The Williams Bros. Soda Works was located at 278 St. John St. in San Jose. David and Thomas manufactured and bottled soda and mineral water at that location from 1871 until David passed away in 1898. Thomas followed him in 1899. Two sons and a daughter ran the soda works after their passing. The bottle listed here should date from the late 1870's into the 1880's.

WILLIAMS BROTHERS,
SODA WATER MANUFACTURERS,
278 ST. JOHN STREET, bet. First and Market Sts.
SAN JOSE, CAL.
Agents Pacific Congress Water and Eastern Cider.

Notes: All but one of the bottles in the gravitator section are embossed on the base with:
GRAVITATING STOPPER MADE BY JOHN MATTHEWS PAT. OCT 11 1864 NEW YORK
The lone hold out is the Marysville Soda Works bottle that is base embossed with the company name. Some of these bottles were in use at the same time as their blob top brothers, if the company used both types of bottles.

SODAS BY GROUPS

TORPEDO SHAPE

ULR ALTING	2
ZAREMBO	95

ROUND BOTTOM

CASSIN'S S.F.	11

MUG BASE SODAS

B & G S.F.	8
C C & B S.F.	12
B.R. LIPPINCOTT	47
W. & B. SHASTA	90

PICTURE SODAS

AMERICAN MIN. WATER "FLAG"	2
AZULE SELTZER WATER "BEAR"	3
BAY CITY SODA WATER "STAR"	5
BREIG & SCHAFER "FISH"	9
CALIF. NATURAL SELTZER B & G "BEAR"	10
CALIF. NATURAL SELTZER H & G "BEAR"	10
CALIF. SODA WORKS FICKEN "EAGLE"	11
CLASSEN & CO. "ANCHORS"	17
COLUMBIA NAPA CO. "EAGLE"	17
COLUMBIA C.C. DALL "SEATED LIBERTY"	17
CROSS "CROSS"	19
COTTLE, POST PORTLAND "EAGLE"	19
EAGLE "EAGLE"	25
EMPIRE VALLEJO "EAGLE"	30
HOFFMAN JOSEPH "LION"	39
NEW ALMADEN VICHY WATER "CREST"	64, 65
NEW LIBERTY "MAN"	66
PACIFIC CONGRESS WATER "DEER"	68, 69
PIONEER SODA WATER "BEAR"	72
PIONEER SODA WORKS "SHIELD"	74
PORTLAND SODA WORKS "EAGLE"	74
E.A. POST PORTLAND "EAGLE"	75
PRIEST MIN. WATER "MAN"	75, 76
C.A. REINERS "MOON & STARS"	77
SAGE'S CONGRESS WATER "DEER"	77
THOMPSON UNION SODA " ACID BOTTLE"	87
WALTER'S NAPA SODA "HORSE SHOE"	88, 89

TEN PIN SHAPE

UNION SODA WORKS S.F.	87

SIDED SODAS

H. BRADER XLCR 8 SIDED	9
CHAMPAGNE MEAD 8 SIDED	14
THE EXCELSIOR WATER 8 SIDED	30
J.N. GERDES 8 SIDED	34
MEAD 8 SIDED	52
McEWIN 10 SIDED	53
NEW ALMADEN 10 SIDED	64

OPEN PONTIL SODAS

BOLEY SACRAMENTO	8
EAGLE SAC CITY	25
LYNDE & PUTNAM S.F.	49
WILLIAMS & SEVERANCE S.F.	91
HENRY WINKLE SAC CITY	92

SLUG PLATE SODAS

BOLEY SAC CITY	8
CHASE & CO. S.F.	13
A.W. CUDWORTH S.F.	21
D.S. & CO. S.F.	24
EAGLE SAC CITY	25
THE EXCELSIOR WATER S.F.	30
GOLDEN GATE YANKEE JIM'S	35
HOGAN & THOMPSON S.F.	39
LIPPINCOTT STOCKTON	47
LYNDE & PUTNAM	49
M. & R. SAC CITY	58
M R & D SAC CITY	58
W & B SHASTA	90

MIKE SOUTHWORTH ADDITIONS

JOHN S. BAKER MINERAL WATER	4 A & B
DEAMER & BORDWELL	23 A & B
GOLDEN WEST SODA	37-A
ASHER S. TAYLOR	85-A

INDEX

A & B	78	EAGLE, motif of	25
AETNA MINERAL WATER	1	EAGLE SODA WORKS	11, 98
AETNA SODA WATER	1	EAGLE WORKS	15, 19
ALMA SODA	54	EASTERN CIDER CO.	26
ALTING, ULR	2	EL-DORADO	26
AMADOR COUNTY SODA WORKS	96	ELLIS & BROTHER	27
AMERICAN MINERAL WATER	2	ELLIS, HENRY H.	26
A.P.	64, 65	EMMITT, T.	27
ASTORG MINERAL WATER	3	EMPIRE SODA WORKS	27, 28, 29, 30, 99
AZULE SELTZER WATER	3	ENGLISH AERATED WATERS	11
B	4, 96	EXCELSIOR SODA WATER	31
B & CO.	44	EXCELSIOR WATER, THE	30
BABB & CO.	4	FARRELL, J.A.	31
BAY CITY SODA WATER	5, 97	FICKEN, H.	11
BELFAST GINGER ALE CO.	6	F.M.	31, 46
B & G	8, 10	FONSECA & CO., D.L.	32
BILLINGS, E.L.	7, 97	FOUNTAIN & TALLMAN	31
BLIVINS & CO., J.I.	97, 104	GEYSER NATURAL BOILED	33
BOLEY & CO.	8	GEYSER SODA	7, 18, 33, 49
BONANZA MINERAL WATER	38	GERDES, J.N.	34
BOWLAND & CRAIG	98	G.G.	32
BRADER & CO., H.	9	GHIRARDELLI'S BRANCH	34
BREIG & SCHAFER	9	GOLDEN GATE	35
BREMENKAMPF & REGLI	9	GOLDEN WEST	36, 37, 38, 70, 83
BRESSON, A.	46	GREENWOOD & MORLEY	37
BURT, W.H.	10	HAAS BROS.	59
CADUC, PHIL	61, 67	H.D.	37
CALIFORNIA NATURAL SELTZER WATER	10	HENDERSON, G.M.	38
CALIFORNIA SELTZER WATER	10	HENRY, ED	45
CALIFORNIA SODA WORKS	11	HERVE & SOMPS	38, 88
CASEY, OWEN	11	H & G	10
CASEY & CRONAN	98	H & H	38
CASSIN'S	11	HIGGINS, E.	39
C C & B	12	HOFFMAN & JOSEPH	39
CERIBELLI, S.	81, 102	HOGAN & THOMPSON	39
CHAMPAGNE MEAD	14	HOLLISTER & CO.	40
CHASE & CO.	13	HOLLISTER SODA WORKS	40
CIRCLE POULSON & CO.	98	HOUGLAND, I.	40, 41
CITY PHARMACY SODA WORKS	98	HUMBOLDT ARTESIAN WATER	41
C & K	15	ITALIAN SODA WATER FACTORY	42
CLASSEN & CO.	16, 17	JACKSON'S NAPA SODA	43, 44, 45, 46
COLUMBIA MINERAL WATER	17	J.B.	42
COLUMBIA SODA WORKS	17	J.H.	84
CONNOLLY, B.F.	45, 60	J.T.	42
CONNOLLY & BRO.	18	JURGENS & PRICE	46
COTTLE, POST & CO.	19	KAPPENMANN	79
C & P	45	KELLY & HANRAHAN	47
C & R	19	KIMBALL & CO.	47
CROSS, motif of	19	L & B	48
CRYSTAL CIDER	20	L, E & J	47
CRYSTAL SODA WATER	20	LELOY, LOUIS	61
CUDWORTH & CO. A.W.	21	LEMONADE	84
DALL, C.C.	17	LEVY BROS.	100
DASCOMBE, JAMES	21	LIPPINCOTT, B.R.	47
DAY & CO., J.	22	LITTON MINERAL WATER	50
DEAMER, W.E.	23, 99	LODTMANN, E. & J.	100
DENHALTER, H.	22	LOS ANGELES SODA WATER	48, 82
DITZ & ELLERKAMP	25	L & V	48
D & M	29		
D.S. & CO.	24, 28		

LYNDE & PUTNAM	49
LYTTON SPRINGS	49
M	50
MADSON, M.	50
MANS, A.	40
MARTINELLI'S	51
MARYSVILLE SODA WORKS	100
MAU & CO., H.	52
MAW & CO., H.	52
McEWIN	53
McG, E.	27
McGEE, B.J.	54
M & D	51
MEAD	52
MERRIAM'S	52
MERRITT & CO.	53
MILLS SELTZER SPRINGS	55
MISENHEIMER & HALL	54
MOISE & CO., C.	55
MONIER & CO., J.	55
MONROE & CO., A.	101
MONROE, J.P.	101
MOONEY, M.	56
MORLEY, C.	56
MORRILL, G.P.	57
M.R.	58
M R & D	58
MT. TAMALPAIS MINERAL WATER CO.	56
NAPA COUNTY	17, 83, 88, 89, 94
NAPA COUNTY SODA SPRINGS	36, 37
NAPA SODA	43, 44, 45, 46, 59, 60, 61, 62, 78, 79, 93
NEVADA CITY SODA WORKS	62
NEVADA SODA WATER CO.	99, 101
NEW ALMADEN MINERAL WATER	64
NEW ALMADEN VICHY WATER	64, 65
NEW CENTURY MINERAL WATER	66
NEW LIBERTY SODA WATER	66
NEYMAN & DRAKE	62
NONPAREIL SODA WATER	66
PACIFIC CONGRESS SPRINGS	68, 69
PACIFIC CONGRESS WATER	67, 68, 69, 77
PACIFIC GINGER BEER	55
PACIFIC GLASS WORKS	54, 67, 95
PACIFIC & PUGET SOUND SODA WORKS	102
PACIFIC SODA WORKS	16, 69
PAILLET, F.	70
PARSONS, T.	70
P. & B.	71, 79
PEARSON BROS.	102
PEARSON SODA WORKS	71
PHILLIPS NAPA MINERAL WATER	72
PHILLIPS SODA SPRINGS	72
PIONEER BROWN & CO.	73
PIONEER SODA WATER CO.	72
PIONEER SODA WORKS	73, 74
PORTLAND SODA WORKS	74
POST, E.A.,	75
PRIEST NATURAL SODA	75, 76
P & W	61
REINER'S & CO., C.A.	77
R & H	76
S & CO., P.J.	103
SAGE'S	69, 77
SAMUEL'S SODA SPRINGS	78, 79
SAN BERNARDINO SODA WORKS	98
SAN FRANCISCO GLASS WORKS	80
SAN JOSE SODA WORKS	81
SAN LUIS OBISPO SODA WORKS	81
SAN RAFAEL SODA WORKS	79
SCHEIDEMANTEL, C.A.	82
SCHNERR & CO.	81
SCHUELER, J.	82
SHAIN & SIMMONS	83
SHOTBOLT, T.	84
SIEBERT, L.	62
SILVA, M.	45
S.L.O. SODA WATER CO.	102
SOMPS, P.	83
SOMPS & MEILLETTE	83
SPARKLING LEMONADE	2
S.P. & CO.	46
STEPHENS & JOSE	103
STOLL, H.W.	48, 82
SULLIVAN, P.J.	103
SUMMIT MINERAL WATER	84
TAHOE SODA SPRINGS	84
TAYLOR & CO.	85
TAYLOR & LOHSE	104, 105
T.A.W.	60
T. & CO.	104
T & H	104
THOMPSON'S MINERAL WATER	87
TOLENAS SODA SPRINGS	86
UNION SODA WORKS	86, 87
VANCE, J.R.	87
VERNON MINERAL WATER	88
VICHY SPRINGS	88, 94
W	59
WALDO, FRANK S.	28
WALTER'S SODA SPRINGS	88, 89
WATSONVILLE CIDER & GINGER ALE	89
W & B	90
W & D	90
WILLIAMS BROS.	105
WILLIAMS & SEVERANCE	91
WILSON, WM.	90
WINKLE, HENRY	92
WINKLER, AUG.	92
W M & D	94
WOOD'S	62, 93
WRIGHT, W.S.	95
WURTZ, HENRY G.	94
W & W	62, 64
X L C R SODA WORKS	9, 94
YOUNG'S MINERAL WATER	94
ZAREMBO	95

ADDITIONS

UKIAH SODA WORKS	86
HAWAIIAN SODA WORKS	40

www.ingramcontent.com/pod-product-compliance
Lightning Source LLC
Chambersburg PA
CBHW061120070526
44583CB00028B/3349